Writing Your Spiritual Autobiography

Writing Your Spiritual Autobiography

Richard B. Patterson, Ph.D.

Allen, Texas

Send all inquiries to:
Thomas More® Publishing
An RCL Company
200 East Bethany Drive
Allen, Texas 75002-3804

Telephone: 800-264-0368 / 972-390-6300
Fax: 800-688-8356 / 972-390-6560

Visit us at: **www.thomasmore.com**
Customer Service E-mail: **cservice@rcl-enterprises.com**

Printed in the United States of America

Library of Congress Control Number: 2002102195

7488 ISBN 88347-488-3

1 2 3 4 5 06 05 04 03 02

To Pinzy,

with gratitude and love.

Thanks for walking with me.

Contents

Acknowledgments

A point I tried to make throughout this book is that each of our spiritual autobiographies can be construed as a pattern of relationships. I mention throughout this book some who blessed my journey. I hope they are not embarrassed by the association.

I would like to thank Debra Hampton and John Sprague of Thomas More Publishing—Debra for believing in my words and John for gently and patiently making them presentable.

My friends and colleagues at Family Therapy Institute of West Texas have been a source of encouragement. Walter Allberg has been a friend for over twenty years and has stood as an impressive example of one not afraid to face his own wounds and bring the resulting learnings into his work. Roberta Pell not only handles the day-to-day worries of my practice but also has brought friendship, kindness, and an impressive ability to make wounded ones feel welcome.

Gerald Bryan, friend and brother since Army days, has walked many, many miles of my journey with me. As I have shared my spiritual struggles, he has encouraged and confronted, all the while in a loving manner. His friendship is one of the great gifts of my life.

My children's impact on me flows throughout these pages. Matt, Becky, Ben, and Andy have inspired me with their own searchings. They are all adults now and I feel privileged to call each of them friend.

I would also like to thank my parents of blessed memory Robert and Genevieve Patterson. My Irish Catholicism which I have come to love and embrace is part of their beautiful legacy to me.

Finally I wish to thank my wife Pinzy to whom this work is dedicated. She is quite simply the finest most decent person I've ever met. If what we are supposed to learn on our journeys has to do with love, then she above all others has shown me the way.

Introduction

I had a frightening thought the other day. I was born in 1948 and have been alive over fifty years. The Catholic faith into which I was born has gone through as much or more turmoil these fifty years as it had seen since the days of Martin Luther. In 1948, Pius XII was pope. Today he is under fire for his attitude toward and possible complicity with the Holocaust. He was replaced by a good, simple man who may very well become a saint in my lifetime. This same man of peasant stock set off a revolution that changed the face of Catholicism forever. He in turn was replaced by a somber man who tried to stem the flow of Catholics beginning to think for themselves. That battle wore him out. He in turn was replaced all too briefly by a man who, given the opportunity, likely would have changed the way Catholics are governed. But he died after only sixty days as pope and was in turn replaced by the unthinkable—a non-Italian. A man of striking contrast who, as I write, looks to be nearing the end of his own tenure as Christ's representative here on earth. A man who has courageously acknowledged the failings of the church he governs.

Through all this change, I have fallen and stumbled along the way, a less-than-model Catholic who has nonetheless tried to make some sense of his faith and church and has tried to determine if indeed the faith of his father and mother is the Way.

In other writings, I have tried to challenge others to strike out on a spiritual path. I have encouraged others to face issues of forgiveness and suffering and to learn to love themselves. I have challenged the hierarchy of the church to share their power before it is too late. I have written longingly of the beauty of simple faith. Wending through all these writings are the bones of my own spiritual story.

There are certainly other stories that are more inspirational. Stories of Damien among the lepers and of Thomas Merton's *Seven Storey Mountain* come to mind. There are biographies and autobiographies of saints and near-saints that more clearly portray a straight and narrow pathway. But there are few stories out there about common seekers—those who struggle to find meaning in empty liturgy, who try to discern what to hold onto and what to jettison from an earlier era that placed great emphasis on sin, who long ago despaired of sainthood and now hope only to hold on long enough to avoid eternal damnation, all the while struggling privately and with some shame with very real doubts.

Our personal faith, I believe, is not made up so much of dogmas as it is of people. People we've known and people we've only read or heard about. This is one's true community of faith. When I think of what I believe, much is in reference to a particular person. My understanding of hell, for example, is in light of words spoken by a saintly Jesuit on a retreat.

Every spiritual autobiography needs a title. Select yours carefully. The title I chose, *Stay With Me,* comes from the theme song from the movie *The Cardinal.* As sung by Frank Sinatra, the lyrics say:

> Should my heart not be humble
> Should my eyes fail to see
> Should my feet sometimes stumble on the way
> Stay with me.

This image remained with me all these years. The hope that in the midst of doubts and of failings, I have not been and will not be alone! The knowledge that if I somehow hang onto my faith, I am indeed not alone but am surrounded by others who own a piece of my faith. Thus, my journey of faith is as much their story as mine.

The writing of one's spiritual autobiography may seem to be an act of self-centeredness to some. To others, it may simply be an interesting exercise that actually serves no useful purpose.

In some twenty-five years of work as a clinical psychologist, I have spent many, many hours listening to what I believe to essentially be spiritual autobiographies unfolding. Themes of suffering and the inevitable question "Why?" Themes of forgiveness. Themes of shame—sin, if you will. What has become clear to me over the years is that at times the simple telling of these stories becomes therapeutic. In addition, examination of and reflection upon these stories can prove helpful. Perhaps a wound has gone unhealed. Perhaps a resentment has festered.

Beyond these broad spiritual themes, many stories have also involved contact with and sometimes struggles with the God of each person's understanding. Sometimes the image of God was in need of healing or at least revision. Sometimes anger was a factor in a person's relationship with God. Often many just seemed lost in their struggle to understand where, if at all, God fit into their lives. I chose a long time ago to struggle along with such persons rather than refer them to a religious professional such as a priest or rabbi. I don't define myself as any sort of religious expert or theologian, but merely as another struggling traveler.

A current popular trend in the world of secular psychotherapy is the notion of narrative therapy—a view of therapy as an enterprise in exploring and expanding one's story. The theory appears to include a commitment to a belief that we each have untapped resources for healing within. These resources become more accessible through the development of one's story. The idea of writing a spiritual autobiography seems completely consistent with the narrative line of thought. Of psychotherapy, Sheldon Kopp writes: "The basic presumption is that the telling of this tale will itself yield good counsel" (*If You Meet the Buddha on the Road, Kill Him!* Bantam: New York, 1976, p. 21).This may be the bottom-line value in working on your own story.

In the pages ahead, I encourage you to develop your own spiritual autobiography. By writing your spiritual autobiography, hopefully you will clarify for yourself first of all exactly what you believe. Not what you have been told by others you should believe. Perhaps you will also discover that what you actually believe and what you thought you believed are a little different, that difference coming to light only when you take the time to examine your beliefs. By talking about the people of your faith and the events of your faith, only then will your true beliefs become clearer. This exercise in clarity and consistency may also be a little humbling, because sometimes we find out that what we believe and what we act out differ.

The enterprise of your spiritual autobiography may also bring into sharper focus the questions with which you are struggling, and possibly generate even more questions.

Your spiritual autobiography can only be of value if you are honest, talking about what actually happened. Don't write to inspire. Write to learn. In this way, you may uncover the greatest gift of a spiritual autobiography—a stronger faith!

It is my hope that the value of writing your spiritual autobiography is not limited by the type of religion, if any, about which you need to write. My own story is organized around Catholicism, and so I am sure this has impact on the language and reflections mentioned ahead. I hope my own metaphor does not confine you for I share Richard Rohr's opinion that "All religion is metaphor" (*Quest for the Grail.* Crossroad: New York, 1997, p. 54).

Throughout each chapter, I have highlighted points for reflection. Take some time with these, as they are intended to provide the "stuff" of your own spiritual story. You may wish to jot down a few notes at these points for further elaboration later on. Space is provided for you to do so.

So dust off your journal. Step on the trail. And be sure to keep your sense of humor in hand.

Reflection: What is the title of *your* spiritual autobiography?

CHAPTER 1

Spiritual Genealogy

Some of us convert to a specific religion, choosing a path in our adult years because it makes sense to us or, perhaps because it is the path of the person with whom we have fallen in love. For others such as me, however, we are born into a particular religion.

As I understand it, my paternal grandfather was a convert. His parents emigrated from Scotland and apparently brought with them a Presbyterian bent, which they passed on to him. At some point, however, presumably after he met my Irish Catholic grandmother, he converted. In those days, so-called mixed marriages were not only frowned upon but viewed as vaguely dangerous for one's soul. What this unifying of faiths did for the souls of my grandparents I do not know. What I do know is that they did not get along. My hunch is that their troubled relationship mirrored some centuries-old animosity between the Scotch and the Irish, an animosity inherited by my father, who also married an Irish Catholic. In any event, the joining of religions even in the midst of conversion did not sit well.

This unrest, I suspect, was passed on to my father, whose own spiritual journey was not a joyous one. Catholic all his life, he focused a great deal on sin, both committing sin and being fearful of its consequences. He came to view his three strokes as "punishment for my sins." This was the faith of my father.

My mother lost her mother in the great flu epidemic of 1919 when she was six years old, one of nine children. My grandfather apparently suffered this loss in a very stoic manner, a feature of Irish Catholicism that I would come to know well. Bearing tragedy became the cornerstone of my mother's faith and was based upon the notion that we all have crosses to bear in life and that some crosses are heavier than others.

My mother also had a fierce devotion to Mary, the mother of Jesus. She would storm heaven and Mary's in-box in particular with petitions for family and friends. After the messages of Fatima and the directive to the Catholic world to pray for "the conversion of Russia," my mother joined in on a daily basis. Some thirty years later when the Soviet Union dissolved, my mother couldn't restrain a triumphant "I told you so!"

I asked my mother once why she prayed so much to Mary. She said, "Only another mother can understand the pain in a mother's heart." When my mother died in 1994, among her things was an impressive collection of rosaries. My favorites are one with the beads imprinted with a shamrock and one with plastic beads of red, blue, green, and yellow.

Reflection: Take a moment and write about the religion with which you grew up. Mention the positive aspects of your parents' faith as well as possible negative influences. If either of your parents used religion to control you (e.g., good ol' guilt trips), write about that as well. Finally, even if religion was not a part of your upbringing, there may have been spiritual influences from either parent. Write about those influences.

This spiritual genealogy sets the tone for your own story. You can then organize your story in a variety of ways. You can simply tell the story in a chronological manner. The value of this approach is that themes may begin to recur. These themes most likely reflect the central issues around which your spiritual story revolves.

You may prefer to organize your spiritual autobiography around certain themes, such as suffering or images of God. For each theme you might write experiences you've had around that theme.

Another way to organize your story is to generate a list of people who've played a role in your story. This list need not be limited to persons you actually know. My own list includes what I call spiritual mentors—persons whom I have never met but whose writings or lives had a profound effect upon me. As examples, I might mention persons ranging from Thomas Merton and Henri Nouwen to playwright Thornton Wilder. Paralleling this list might also be a listing of significant spiritual writings. Don't list what you think is *supposed* to be on your list; rather, put down whatever actually had impact.

Before we leave the theme of spiritual genealogy, there is another facet of what we inherit that needs discussion. Most of us at some point early in our journeys experience both curses and blessings. Curses are statements made to us that haunt us. We may expend great energy trying to undo the curse. Or we may feel that the impact of the curse is inevitable and so we simply give in to it. I have known persons struggling with curses such as "You'll never amount to anything" or "You're nothing but a slut" or "You're gonna be a bum just like your no-good father." In my own case, I was cursed by my seventh grade teacher who told me (among other things) that I was "a villain" and "a leader in badness" and that as a result my eternal salvation was very much in question.

Fortunately, though, we are sometimes also blessed. In other words, we may have been fortunate enough to have had someone affirm us, point us toward our gifts or, most especially, we may have experienced unconditional love. These, too, can be powerful messages that pull us through dark times.

Reflection: Think of ways in which you were cursed and blessed as a child.

CHAPTER 2

On Suffering

I am convinced that while my mother carried me she stormed heaven with prayer. She was frightened. My older sister had been born with spina bifida and died after three days. In those days, there was no way of knowing what was coming when you were pregnant. No ultrasound. No amniocentesis. You just prayed that whatever came out would have the right parts in the right places. My older sister didn't. As such, when my mother carried me, she had no idea what to expect.

Well, I turned out OK, more or less. I like to think I was a source of relief to my mother when I popped out with everything in the right place. But during my second year, my mother was again pregnant. There is a picture of me with my mother during this time. I have just plucked a pear from my grandfather's tree and am looking at my mother who is smiling back. But she is pregnant and there is a bit of anxiety in her eyes. My younger sister Linda was born about two months before my third birthday. She, too, had spina bifida. She lived four months, spending her last days in St. Joseph's Hospital.

We lived up the street from St. Joseph's Hospital, a truly mysterious place. It was a hospital first of all for unwed mothers, young women who were at times the subject of "fires of hell" sermons at the nearby Catholic women's college. It was also a home for children who were retarded or worse and could not live at home or did not have a home. We'd often see many of these kids outside playing. Inside there was a ward for those children who could not play—the ones with hydrocephalus and other horrifying deformities. In high school once as a social service project we toured St. Joseph's. When we came to that ward, one young man had to leave so he could throw up.

So St. Joseph's was a final stop for my sister and others of—what?—God's mistakes? My sister spent her final days in that ward and then, to quote my mother, became an angel.

Spina bifida is a congenital disease in which the spinal column does not fully close. Hydrocephalus can be one of the results. Nowadays children can survive, albeit with significant impairment. It is not a disease you get from smoking too many cigarettes or eating too much chocolate. You are born with it. No choice. No chance to undo the damage.

And so my two sisters set the stage for what would become a central struggle of my Catholic faith. What's the deal, God? What gives here? Not one but two kids born with a horrible deformity that killed them both? Did some Patterson somewhere offend you or what?

Reflection: In general, what kinds of suffering have you encountered which have not made sense to you?

The lives and deaths of my sisters were, of course, never discussed. I say "of course" because we were after all quite Irish Catholic and so adopted the standard ethnic position of silence. In fact, I learned of their existence only after paging through the family Bible one day after I'd learned to read. These were the days when family Bibles were also the holders of family records. And so on one page that listed significant births were the names Linda and Patricia. Patricia was listed as being born on December 12, 1946, and dying December 15, 1946. Linda was listed as being born in December of 1951, followed by the words in my mother's handwriting "Died in April." So it goes. This was where I first found these two girls who would have such a profound effect on my spiritual journey. My mother would answer questions I had. My father never spoke about them. And I spent many years wondering. What happened to them? What would life have been like if they had lived? And most especially, at some level even when I was young, why did this happen?

Whether my father believed that what happened to my sisters was a punishment for his sins, I do not know. My mother never questioned it. Life was made up of crosses to bear, she believed. You picked yours up and didn't argue. Neither my father's nor my mother's position ever worked for me.

In subsequent years, I was dogged by the "why" question. Not just about my sisters but about any suffering that seemed senseless. Why did this very good family lose a child to Reye's syndrome? Why do children die at all, much less of horrible, disfiguring diseases such as cancer? I have heard this preached about many times, the ultimate answer being, "It's a mystery." A Mys-ter-y A Mys-ter-y. That answer over time began to sound like something out of a Gilbert and Sullivan operetta.

Sometime in 1988 I had a dream about my younger sister. I dreamed of her as a healthy adult. Like me, she was tall and thin. In the dream, she had a drinking problem and I was taking her for help. I took her to the door of the treatment center then let her walk through. It was as vivid a dream as I've ever had, the kind where you wake up believing it to have happened. In that split instant between sleep and waking I thought, "A mistake has been made. She's alive. My sister's alive. She's out there somewhere." Then wakefulness took charge and I realized it was a dream. Some weeks later my wife mentioned my dream to my mother. This opened up the reality of my sisters for acknowledgement, so that when my mother was ready to die, she said, "My bags are packed and I'm going to see my girls."

C. S. Lewis wrote that Christianity creates the problem of pain: "In a sense, it (Christianity) creates, rather than solves, the problem of pain, for pain would be no problem unless, side by side with our daily experience of this painful world, we had received what we think a good assurance that ultimate reality is righteous and loving" (*The Problem of Pain.* Macmillan: New York, 1962, p. 24). By this he meant that, once we posit the existence of a loving God, then we are put in a position of trying to explain senseless suffering. No loving God? Then senseless suffering doesn't have to make sense. In a godless world, ugliness and pain happen.

But this is not what I was taught. I was taught that God loves us. (Mostly. Actually, my early exposure to God was a bit more of a mixed bag. God both loves and punishes.)

Jewish people, too, have been challenged to make sense of suffering. The question "Where was God in the death camps?" has not only troubled many Jews, but others as well. Where was God in the death camps? And if and when God does show up, what is it that we expect him/her to do about the suffering? Do we expect a miracle, or do we content ourselves with God's compassion, accepting, as Anne Lamott does, that "God isn't there to take away our suffering or our pain but to fill it with his or her presence"? (*Traveling Mercies: Some Thoughts on Faith.* Pantheon: New York, 1999, p. 241).

Many of us, Jews and Christians alike, take comfort in the notion that the scales are balanced in the next life. In discussing Jewish belief about suffering, Joseph Telushkin writes: "The only possible explanation for God allowing so much suffering and injustice is that there is another dimension of existence where there is redress" (*Jewish Wisdom.* William Morrow & Co., New York, 1994, p. 276). In other words, not only are we rewarded, but the guys who did us dirty eventually pay up. We make sense of our suffering by putting a theological twist to the modern myth, "What goes around comes around."

I remember, though, a story told by Abraham Twerski (*Generation to Generation: Personal Reflections of a Chassidic Legacy.* Traditional Press: Brooklyn, 1985, p. 13). In the story, he describes a man in a prison. This man's job was to turn a wheel embedded in a wall. This is all he did for years. He dealt with this task by convincing himself that on the other side of the wall was a great and important machine that his turning helped to operate. Many of us deal with suffering in the same way. We believe that it makes some sense in the larger scheme of things. Indeed, the great psychiatrist

Victor Frankl stated that this quality is one facet of being human. There is much suffering about which we can do nothing. But we can make some decision as to how we face such suffering. Frankl wrote: "Man is not free from conditions, be they biological or psychological or sociological in nature. But he is and always remains free to take a stand toward these conditions; he always retains the freedom to choose his attitude toward them" ("The philosophical foundations of logotherapy" in *Psychotherapy and Existentialism.* Simon and Schuster: New York, 1967, p. 3).

Reflection: What different stances have you taken toward suffering? What stances of others have you especially admired?

Frankl helps me make sense of what we can do in the face of suffering. But I am still left with the question of how such suffering adds up, and I am bothered by the nagging doubt that on the other side of the wall is—nothing!

I have read C. S. Lewis. I have read Annie Dillard. I have read Zen Buddhists. Anyone who offers the hope of some insight. Early on, I read Harold Kushner's wonderful *When Bad Things Happen to Good People.* (Avon: New York, 1997). Rabbi Kushner, like Victor Frankl, writes with the authority of one who has suffered senseless events. Kushner offers the provocative notion that perhaps God is not in charge of everything—that some things just happen.

Now, I had gotten clear the idea that some suffering, e.g., being gunned down in a senseless school shooting, resulted from the freely chosen acts of others. We are a self-destructive species. But I struggled with things like my sisters' birth defects. Kushner suggests that indeed such things just happen. I have struggled with this concept ever since I first read it in the early 1980s. Where, then, is God in the midst of such suffering. Clearly present, say Kushner and others. But as a comfort, not as a cause.

What I have begun to realize is that I let go reluctantly of the notion of a God who is all-powerful, who is responsible for everything. There is a part of me that wants it all to make sense, even if I don't like the answer. As Annie Dillard says, "If God does not cause everything that happens, does God cause anything that happens? Is God completely out of the loop?" (*For the Time Being.* A. Knopf: New York, 1999, p. 167).

I cling sometimes to the notion Harold Kushner rejects. He suggests one view that posits life to be like the backside of a knitted wall hanging. What we see is various strands of string. But God sees the other side, the meaningful pattern. I cling to a hope that this is so.

And so some fifty years later I still don't know why my sisters were born with spina bifida. I don't know why my parents were dealt such blows. I'm not even sure where God is or was in the midst of all this. What I do know is that going quietly does not work for me. I take great comfort from my friend Job.

William Safire observes that "the Book of Job is not a weary resignation to life's unfairness. Rather, it is a sustained note of defiance" (*The First Dissident: The Book of Job in Today's Politics.* Random House: New York, 1992, p. xiv). Job, you may remember, was a good and decent man who suffered as a result of a deal made between God and Satan. He lost everything. Worse yet, his buddies turned on him, telling him he'd surely sinned or simply wasn't praying hard enough. Job clearly suffered senselessly. And he blamed God for the suffering. In fact, he was angry with God. He even demanded that God show up and make an accounting of Himself. Granted, God resorted to some special effects and put Job in his place. But God never punished Job for being angry. As William Safire says, "The answering and not the answer is what finally silenced Job and possibly satisfied him . . . What God did was to show up" (*Ibid,* p. 74). Now, *this* is a comfort!

I have been told by some very good people to not question God. Sorry, folks, that doesn't work for me. Whatever God I am able to believe in has to be one who will allow me to be angry. I once read a beautiful book by Pierre Wolff titled *May I Hate God?* (Paulist Press, 1983).

Wolff's answer is a resounding "Yes." He draws a beautiful metaphor. We are taught God is a loving Father/Mother. What loving parent, if his/her child were angry at him/her, would not want to hear about it? "Tell me what you're upset about. Let's talk about it. See if we can't straighten things out. Don't withdraw into silence!" This may be a God I can approach.

Reflection: Have you ever been angry with God? Write about it.

CHAPTER 3

On Prayer

A second spiritual theme emerged in my preschool years. My mother was a great believer in prayer. Her prayer was almost entirely selfless. I nonetheless got the idea that I could pray for things for myself. Stuff. Thus, when I was four or five, and after being turned down by my parents, I prayed for a pony.

My parents, mainly my mother, had tried reasoning. We didn't have a backyard to keep a pony in, she would say. Or it would cost too much for upkeep. I was not to be deterred. I began to pray for a pony for Christmas.

My mother prayed a lot. She prayed for ill relatives. She prayed for missionaries. She prayed for the conversion of Russia. She prayed for my brother and me and then, after I was married and a father, for my wife and children. She had a deep belief in the power of prayer.

I can remember an early doubt I had about prayer. It had to do with two Catholic schools playing each other in some sporting event. Did God choose sides? Was the winning school a reflection of better praying? Later it occurred to me to wonder whether God was particularly interested in the outcome of an athletic competition.

Someone once said that at deathbeds and in foxholes there are many unanswered prayers. This issue of prayer obviously overlaps with my struggle about suffering, because unanswered prayers, according to some, reflect God's will. And, as Garth Brooks sings, sometimes God does indeed seem to know what he/she is doing.

But I have also dealt with many who prayed incessantly for a miracle, only to lose a loved one to something like cancer, whereas someone else's family member recovers. Is there a trick here? Some sort of incantation that, if I figure it out, gets my prayers answered? Sadly, many persons in such a situation blame themselves, lamenting, "Perhaps I didn't pray hard enough or correctly." I have to reject the notion that there is a special formula or fervor that makes prayer work but that we have to guess at the formula. Such a God would be a cruel one.

What I have learned is that some people have a marvelous capacity to accept unanswered prayers calmly and without bitterness. I truly admire this. It reflects a depth of belief in God, in God's benevolence, and in God's will. But my heart aches when I listen to a very good woman say that, because her child died, this must mean that she did not pray correctly or that the sum total of her past sins canceled out any chance of her prayers being answered.

Do I still pray? In general, yes. I pray for good things for my wife and children. I pray when I am afraid. (Remember: There are no atheists in foxholes!) And I have learned that prayers of gratitude help me feel more at peace. I don't pray much about money matters anymore because I really don't think God is interested in money problems. If anything, God is probably wary of money matters. Rich people don't like to be reminded of what Jesus had to say about their chances of getting into heaven.

And if you haven't guessed by now, no, I did not get my pony.

Reflection: What role has prayer played in your life? What types of experiences have you had? And what about unanswered prayers?

CHAPTER 4

On Sin

One of my earliest memories of Catholicism comes from the fact that we lived very near to a church and rectory. I remember walking past that rectory and that seeing numerous priests sitting on the porch after dinner. Five or more priests at a time. Such numbers in a parish are unheard of now.

My formal religious education began in the first grade. I attended a parochial Catholic school across the street. These were still the days when many parishes had their own schools, a likely carryover from immigration days when ethnic groups took care of their own. In any event, this school was run by a religious order of women who wore dark blue habits with uncomfortable-looking devices that completely covered their heads. They also carried rosary beads, *big* rosary beads dangling at their sides. For seven of my first eight years, I would have one of these sisters as my teacher.

The religious teaching of my early years was heavy on sin. In other words, a great emphasis was placed on what to avoid doing. This isn't to say that there was never a discussion of doing good for others, etc., but there was a strong emphasis on avoiding going to hell, a task which, to people like me with a knack for getting into trouble, was a daunting one. And, at times, a task with disturbing implications.

One spiritual task of my journey, then, has been to make peace with the nuns. Some of these women unfortunately dealt with us in ways that, if not cruel, were at least not very enlightened. I recall, for instance, that one of the many times I got into trouble (this time talking in the lunch line), after being punished for a while, I was directed to go home and write a letter to Santa Claus asking him to bypass my house. This, to a six-year-old child, was truly devastating. My mother, in a moment I've grown to appreciate over time, told me to just ignore sister. Nothing further was ever said about the matter.

At this point, the reader may be thinking, "Oh No! More horror stories of Catholic grade schools." And indeed, for years I blamed many of my woes, spiritual and otherwise, on those women. However, while in graduate school,

I attended a talk given by a local priest. I took it upon myself to mention how misguided I believed these women to be. The priest gently confronted me by suggesting that it was equally misguided to blame women from twenty years ago for my current spiritual struggles. This comment started the process of letting go of hard feelings I had held onto for all that time.

Helpful, too, is Leo Booth's work on religion abuse. Father Booth describes situations of various degrees in which persons invoke religious tenets in a way that can only be viewed as emotionally abusive. Somehow being able to label some of what happened to me and others as religion abuse was healing.

Reflection: Have you had any experiences that might qualify as religious abuse, i.e., people using the tenets of religion to control or demean you? What has the impact of such experiences been on your spiritual journey?

The religious teaching of those early years was heavy on sin, and sexual sin at that. I recall a day in the sixth grade when Sister Leonard (not her real name) dismissed the girls to another class so that she could "have a talk with the boys." We were sure this was going to be *the talk.* Instead, after a few moments, Sister went into a Dennis Miller-style rant about—tree houses. The impact on us boys was significant. None of us had a tree house so we clearly felt we were missing something, although we weren't quite sure what. Tree houses were nonetheless defined as "an occasion of sin." For some, such teachings maintain power well into later years. Others, after a process of reflection and study, come to a conclusion that runs contrary to the teachings of our youth and change behavior accordingly. In other words, such persons choose to sin bravely. To me, sinning bravely is a true act of courage in which we conclude that a certain course of action in fact is not sinful and follow this course in spite of the accompanying old-tape fear and guilt.

Reflection: What have your experiences been with the concept of sin? Are you bothered by what might be considered "old tapes" as far as sin is concerned? Have you had experiences with "sinning bravely"?

Much of my early spiritual life, then, was tinged with fear. What we Catholics were told is that certain sins, most notably mortal ones, were a serious matter. Of what were we afraid? Clearly many of us were afraid of going to hell. What condemned the sinner to hell was if he/she were to die without confessing those sins. This threat raised interesting moral questions even to us grade schoolers. For example, if I was on my way to confession and was hit by a car and died just before going into the church, *even though I was going to confession,* did I still earn eternal damnation? The black-and-white thinking at that time would seem to say, "Sorry, Charley!"

In any case, fear of going to hell was a major force of the Catholicism of the time. Mind you, much like the threat of capital punishment, it didn't necessarily deter me from sin. It just made me in a mighty big hurry to get to confession once I did sin. Such thinking stayed with me a long time and still on occasion raises its head. A saintly Jesuit helped my thinking about hell. But that story is for later.

Hell and heaven, then, were a major focus of my grade school spirituality and approximately in that order. My flirting with hell was enhanced by the reality that I was a bit of what would nowadays be categorized as a behavioral problem. In those days, however, diagnostic nomenclature was limited to good versus bad or more elaborate forms such as "villain" and "leader in badness." Falling into this category was distinguished in a variety of ways, including having to stand in the supply closet, having to move one's desk to the front corner of the room or, even worse, out into the hallway, having to stay after school and, for the true incorrigibles, staying after school for a half hour, then spending the hour or so after in the basement of the convent (the nuns' home next door to the school). Such were the marks of those of us destined for damnation.

Most of what I got into trouble for was mild by modern standards—talking in class, the occasional fight, playing hooky a time or two. Once, however, I did tell one of the sisters to go to hell. She was apparently so shocked that she simply told me to sit down at my desk. All of this relatively harmless behavior of a hyperactive kid did, however, give me a fairly strong sense of being bad. Yet I never confessed to talking in class or playing hooky. Some real confusion about sin was taking root.

Reflection: What have your experiences been with the ideas of heaven and hell? What beliefs do you hold to at present?

CHAPTER 5

On Mysticism

During my grade school years, a powerful notion grew within me, blossoming sometime in the eighth grade. It grew not out of guilt or fear but out of a desire to be of service. Thus it was that sometime in the eighth grade, after serving Benediction, I announced to Father Andriuska that I wanted to be a priest.

First a word on Father Andriuska. He was the chaplain at the local home for elderly sisters. He lived there and toiled day and night on their behalf. A hump-backed man who apparently would have been six-foot-eight if standing straight, he mentored me for several years and offered a lasting example of tireless service. My friend Joe Mellody and I spent much time helping him with various tasks around the center. We also served Mass regularly. Father George died suddenly when I was a junior in high school, leaving a great void in my spiritual world.

Now about being a priest. In those days, becoming a priest was greatly admired. There were frequent talks at school about "having a vocation," something which was considered to be a gift from God given to a special few. You either had one or you didn't. Not that other callings in life were bad or even inferior, we were told. It was just that the calling to religious life was a special calling indeed. And I was convinced, at age thirteen, that I had it.

As with so much else in my spiritual journey, people were a central part of my desire to be a priest. There were numerous priests, real and fictional, who had inspired me, Father George and Father Robert Gibson, a parish priest, being two in particular. Damien among the lepers. Father Dismas Clark and his convicts. The priests portrayed by Burgess Meredith and Tom Tryon in *The Cardinal.* I was also deeply inspired by films ranging from *Ben Hur* to the gentle *Miracle of Marcellino.* All these people and films shared a piece of my desire to become a priest.

There were books that I read—John Farrow's book about Damien, Edwin O'Conner's Pulitzer Prize-winning *The Edge of Sadness* (a book which

I recently reread and perceived much differently), and *The Keys of the Kingdom* by A. J. Cronin. These people and writers all owned a piece of my vocation.

But I believe the greatest influence on my desire to become a priest was an early grasping of what I now believe to be one of the strengths of Catholicism—its grasp of the mystical dimension of spirituality. As a child, I had some experiences in which I felt God was very near. These were powerful events, ones I've never forgotten and, nowadays, long for. I did not have visions or hear God's Voice. I just had a strong sense of God's presence. These experiences pulled me toward the priesthood. The desire for a sense of mystical connection has remained a key element of my journey.

This, I have come to believe, is one of the strengths of Catholicism, a deep appreciation for the mystical side of life. Are mystical experiences limited to some encounter with the God of one's understanding? I don't think so. I believe we touch the mystical side when we sense a deep connection with someone or some facet of God's creation, such as finding God in a neighbor's face or suddenly encountering a gentle deer on a remote trail. Rabbi Heschel speaks of the ineffable: "To become aware of the ineffable is to part company with words" (*I Asked for Wonder: A Spiritual Anthology of Abraham Joshua Heschel.* Crossroad: New York, 1990, p.2). Psychiatrist Carl Jung talks of the numinous. Naturalist John Muir speaks thus about the mystical connection: "I only went out for a walk and finally concluded to stay out til sundown, for going out, I found, was really going in" (*The Wilderness World of John Muir.* Houghton Mifflin: Boston, 1954, p. 311).

I do not claim to be a mystic yet I have had some mystical experiences ranging from the above-mentioned encounter with a deer to the first glance I had of each of my newborn children. My understanding of mysticism is greatly helped by Loren Eisley when he writes: "The convenient label 'mystic' is, in our day, readily applied to men who pause for simple wonder . . ." ("The illusion of two cultures" in *The Star Thrower.* Harcourt Brace Javonovich: New York, 1970, pp. 272–73). This, then, may be the doorway for many of us into the mystical realm. Most of us have experienced wonder—those events that we witness and in which we participate but which elude words to capture their full impact. They may be events of great transitions. Witnessing birth. Being present at the moment of death. Or perhaps they have included encounters with breathtaking facets of creation.

Mystical encounters and wondrous moments, however, are not limited to meetings with the powers of light, for the numinous domain also contains,

I believe, darkness. Thus, experiences of wordless horror are also mystical. Was it not a moment of wondrous horror when we watched the space shuttle *Challenger* explode? Were we not struck speechless on September 11, 2001?

Reflection: Write about mystical experiences you have had, even if they do not have a specific sense of God about them. Include in your reflections your experiences of wonder, and include horrifying wonder.

I emerged from my grade school years with two strong but contrasting, almost contradictory, themes—the power of the mystical domain and yet a great focus on sin. Polarities. The agony and the ecstasy.

My early Catholic education was not well grounded in any relationship with the Bible. This, I believe, is not uncommon for many Catholics. As such, I did not emerge from childhood with a good knowledge about Scripture. But I did emerge with certain stories that stayed with me. There was the story about Jesus getting angry in the Temple, a story that seemed to be at odds with the teaching I'd received that anger was bad. There was the story of Dismas the Good Thief, crucified with Jesus, who was told that he was about to receive an eternal inheritance. The story of Dismas long fascinated me, perhaps because it gives hope to us as sinners. There was the Song of Songs (which actually did not get talked about a whole lot) that seemed to affirm sexual loving. There was the Agony in the Garden where Christ seemed to struggle for a moment with doubt. All these stories stayed with me, perhaps because I needed them for the road ahead.

Reflection: What were the sacred writings of your religious tradition? What impact have they had on your journey?

While Catholicism may have been weak on Scripture, it was strong on ritual. And the central ritual was, of course, the Mass.

I have heard the Mass referred to as an act of cannibalism. I have heard it referred to as an act of idol worship. In my early years I had a poor understanding of the ritual, the center of which was the Eucharist. We were told that at the Consecration of the Mass, the bread and wine became the Body and Blood of Christ. Not a symbol but the actual Body and Blood! This, in my early years, seemed to be something very sacred. In fact, it was something I did not and to this day do not understand.

Ritual can play a key role in our journeys. They help us connect with tradition. They provide an organized way of attempting to grasp elusive beliefs. And at a more human level, "Rituals bestow protected time and space to stop and reflect on life's transformations" (Imber-Black, Evan, and Janine Roberts. *Rituals for our Times: Celebrating, Healing, and Changing our Lives and our Relationships.* Harper Collins: San Francisco, 1992, p. 3). When I was young, given the arrogance of youth, I would scoff at the Irish Catholic rituals created around death. But in time, when my own parents died, I found comfort in these rituals. The Irish wake, I saw, was more than an excuse to get drunk. It brought friends and family together in a particular way that brought great comfort.

Reflection: Were there any rituals in your own tradition? Did any elude your understanding?

Many of us boys did more than bear witness to the puzzling ritual of Mass. We participated in it as altar boys. In general, if you went to a Catholic school, you were expected to at least attempt to become an altar-boy. Nonetheless, there was a sense in those altar boy days of being a part of something sacred. Brian Doyle's poetic words capture it best: "I remember the dark scent of the church at dawn, the dense purple light, the smells of incense and cigars and dust. I remember the dry shuffling of shoes as communicants shuffled toward the Host. I remember the twisted faces of saints in the windows. . . . I remember the groaning organ and the reverberating yowl of an infant being baptized in the knave. I remember the stiff black cloth under which you hid all desire and personality as you prepared to assist at a miracle you did not and could not understand. . . ." (Doyle, Brian, "Altar Boy," American Scholar. Spring 1997) In essence, Doyle reflects that being an altar boy allowed us front-row seats at a mystical experience.

My final year in grade school was marked by other more human events. Teaching younger boys how to serve Mass. Playing on our school basketball team. Struggling through the throes of puberty. And, sometime after my fourteenth birthday, drinking. It would be years before I learned that, at a basic level, my interests in the mystical life and my attraction to alcohol were strongly connected.

Reflection: Were there any rituals in your own tradition? Did any elude your understanding?

CHAPTER 6

On Thinking and Doubting

When I began high school in 1962, the faint rumblings of change were just beginning to be felt within the Catholic Church. Some elements of tradition, however, were still evident. One of these traditions was the value and power of an education by Jesuits.

The Society of Jesus was founded by a warrior and had developed a strong tradition of intellectual acuity and educational excellence. Two goals were clearly elucidated in the Jesuit philosophy of education: learn to study and learn to think. The Jesuits, I found, were not afraid to think. It was the Jesuits who taught me that there is no such thing as a dangerous idea.

My history of behavior problems did not evaporate in the presence of Jesuits, although they were tempered somewhat by rumors that our headmaster Father Bernard McIlhenny was a former Golden Gloves champion. But there was a certain pride involved with attending the local Jesuit high school.

These men by and large fit a pre-Vatican II picture of priests—tough men, many of whom were veterans of either the Second World War or the Korean War. Priests of this era were more like football coaches. Many of them also were hard drinkers.

Jesuit education in those days was not coeducational. As such, our contact with girls was extremely limited. This, I believe, was a major flaw in that system, but one consistent with the residual thinking about dealing with sexual impulses. Out of sight, out of mind was the basic thought. If girls weren't around, you'd be less likely to be "distracted," more able to focus on your studies. Psychology being what it is, however, the exact opposite effect was probably what actually happened.

In any event, in September of 1962, I entered the local Jesuit High school and met some men who would profoundly affect my journey.

During my first year, our religion class was taught by John FitzPatrick, S.J., a man who, according to rumor, had been a paratrooper. Father FitzPatrick early on proposed a notion that was then truly shocking: He suggested that we not take everything literally that was in the *Baltimore Catechism.*

The *Baltimore Catechism* was the mainstay of Catholic education at that time. It presented basic truths of the Catholic faith in question-and-answer format, thus communicating a certain "black-and-white" flavor. Questions and answers were to be memorized, then recited by rote upon request. This was the backbone of religious education. Questions and ponderings were not encouraged. Everything in the *Baltimore Catechism* was to be simply accepted "on faith."

Father FitzPatrick's directive was more than a little alarming. He pointed out, for example, that the discussion of the effects of "impure acts" was just a little inaccurate, and was so forthright as to tell us pubescent boys that, despite what the *Catechism* said, masturbation did not cause brain damage or insanity. This nowadays can seem ludicrous, but such were the scare tactics of the day. But at Father FitzPatrick's suggestion, the door was open for me to question, even to have doubts. If things in the *Baltimore Catechism* were to be examined, even questioned . . . this was truly a revolutionary notion.

Doubts, you see, had been discouraged, even viewed as weak, if not downright sinful. But here was a man of God encouraging me to *think* about what I believed. This mustard seed of wisdom would in time allow me not only to have doubts but also to welcome them. It prepared me to understand words from the likes of Rabbi David Wolpe: "Belief without elements of terror and doubt is fairy tale, not faith" (*The Healer of Shattered Hearts: A Jewish View of God.* Penguin: New York, 1990, p.7).

Reflection: Have there been times of doubting during your spiritual journey? With what doubts have you struggled?

Somewhere during these years, I noticed more clearly Saint Thomas the Apostle, a man who became one of my spiritual mentors. Many look down on Thomas, viewing him as inferior because he longed for a sign to bolster his faith. The story is basically that Jesus had risen from the dead, but Thomas would not believe it unless he was able to touch Jesus' wounds. Jesus appears, Thomas sees him, and Jesus offers to Thomas the opportunity to touch his wounds. Thomas is appropriately humble. Jesus then adds particular praise for those who believe without a sign. *But He never condemns Thomas!*

Some years later, I saw in this story Jesus' deep love for Thomas. Have you ever suffered a scarring injury or gone through a significant surgery? Would you share your scars with someone, much less invite someone to touch them? This is a very intimate communication. Yet Jesus extended this offer to Thomas so that he might be more secure in his beliefs. Jesus loved Thomas this much!

So for me, Thomas became a source of hope in the midst of my doubts. Maybe those of us who struggle to believe are not lost.

I have always admired people of simple faith. These are people who are not dogmatic, who do not project a "better than" attitude regarding their beliefs. These people of simple faith are humble folk who do not impose their beliefs on others but who conduct themselves in accord with a few straightforward beliefs that, by and large, they do not question. I truly envy such simple faith. I do not use the term *simple* to imply some lack of intellectual power. Rather, it is meant to imply a lack of complications, for I have also seen that the dark side of a thoughtful approach to faith can be a good deal of confusion and needless complexity.

Reflection: Have you known people of simple faith? What impact have they had on your journey?

During my high school years, the full impact of Vatican II was being felt in that priests and sisters began a fairly massive exodus from their religious lives into the world of the laity. In Jesuit training, men would serve a period of time as a "scholastic" during which they would teach and live in religious community. They were, however, several years away from ordination. Of the fifteen or so scholastics I knew during my high school years, only three would ever be ordained. One of the priests who left during that time was actually the ranking Jesuit of the Maryland province. His departure planted a question in many minds: "Maybe I can leave. Maybe I can be just as good a person in another lifestyle."

I had not yet parted company with the idea of becoming a priest. In fact, during my senior year, I applied to and was accepted by the Holy Cross fathers. I have to admit that I was drawn to them in part because they were affiliated with Notre Dame. But I had visited their seminary in Massachusetts and was drawn to the quiet and to the intense spiritual focus. The vocations director Father Frank Gartland was also an old-school type of priest, a good spiritual man who enriched my journey. Unfortunately, I also had exposure to the emerging dark side of celibacy at that seminary when a seminarian with whom I was rooming tried to molest me.

However I continued to be exposed to positive role models of priesthood. I first learned of Father Charles Dismas Clark through the film *The Hoodlum Priest.* Father Clark worked in St. Louis on behalf of the incarcerated and developed a halfway house movement for them. His story allowed me to fully embrace Saint Dismas the Good Thief. Dismas became my second significant saint.

According to legend, Dismas was crucified with Christ. While they were dying, as recorded by Saint Luke, another criminal began to mock Jesus. Dismas cut him short, then turned to Jesus and asked to be remembered. Jesus uttered incredible words: "Today you will be with me in paradise." This story of Dismas has stood ever since as a beacon of hope for me and for others. I have, over the years, given religious medals of Saint Dismas to those waging special wars against poor self-esteem. Dismas had truly hit bottom yet was promised eternal reward. This ought to encourage all of us.

The other facet of faith that paralleled the permission to doubt was the emphasis Jesuits place on thinking. I was taught, then encouraged, to think about what I believed. This may not seem like much of an insight, but in those days (and to some extent still) there were elements in various organized religions that stated that good faith does not question but merely accepts in a childlike manner.

Most religious traditions are replete with thinkers—men and women who analyzed the tenets of their faith either to understand them better or to attempt to explain them more clearly to others. Sometimes thinkers are condemned and persecuted. Witness the likes of Galileo. Thinkers tend to be attacked when the fruit of their thinking challenges the party line. Teilhard de Chardin is a case in point. de Chardin was a brilliant anthropologist-priest (a Jesuit!) whose complex theories of evolution were roundly condemned in the 1940s and 1950s with de Chardin being silenced. Subsequent to his death, his works eventually were reconsidered, and today he is regarded as a mystic and visionary.

I do understand why some authorities discourage thinking about one's beliefs, for if you think, then you may question. And if you question, you may reject. Or, at the very least, you may discover that you really don't understand what something means. Rabbi Wolpe's words are a comfort: "Indifference, not anguished denial, is the true enemy of faith" (*Ibid,* p. 171).

Reflection: Are there any religious beliefs to which you aspire but about which you rarely think? List them.

There are many tenets of my Catholicism that I now realize I don't understand. Haven't the foggiest. Body and Blood of Christ? Don't have a clue! This doesn't mean, however, that I automatically reject such notions. Only that I need to think about them.

Thinking, too, challenges us to lay claim to what we believe. Thinking in essence allows us to confront the question, "Why do you believe what you believe?"

Reflection: How do you approach such a question at this time?

Alcohol consumption became an increasing part of my life in high school. In those days it was a sign of manhood to be able to consume huge amounts of beer. Given that I was an otherwise insecure soul, I developed some skill at this. By the time I was a senior, some of my friends and I were drinking like alcoholics.

In my last two years of high school, I was also greatly influenced by Father John Herrity, S.J. Father Herrity had originally been our math teacher, but by the time I was a senior he taught religion and also mentored the sodality. Sodalities to this point were social service organizations in many Catholic schools. Father Herrity introduced, however, a revolutionary idea. Why not join our sodality with that of the local Catholic all-*girls* school? Father Herrity, it seemed, sensed the twisted view of women that our education gave us and took it upon himself to try to offset that. So the halls of our high school rang with the voices of girls.

Beyond this, Father Herrity had the courage to guide us into areas of thought clearly at odds with Catholic thinking. During these years, a controversy evolved known as the "Death of God" controversy. Philosophers questioned the validity or necessity of the concept of God. Rather than blindly condemning such thinking, Father Herrity encouraged us to *examine it!* Thus, I found myself reading Fredrich Nietzsche. Not that I understood him, but this exposure did introduce me to the notion that ideas were to be examined, that we should avoid what is known in AA circles as "contempt prior to investigation."

Reflection: Have you encountered ideas in your spiritual journey which you were afraid to examine? What "dangerous ideas" did you face head-on?

CHAPTER 7

On Sex and Sexuality

My years with the Jesuits were not all blissful. My behavior problems continued and I became a frequent participant of what was known as "Jug" (judgment under God), an after-school "program" for students in trouble. The same faces tended to show up.

By the same token, a few well-meaning Jesuits tried to engage us in the joys of meditation, most likely within the framework of Saint Ignatius's *Spiritual Exercises.* I was a dismal failure. I would try concentrating on, say, a holy card, but very quickly my mind drifted to other topics such as the World Series or the fine features of actress Carol Lynley. I have to admit that, try as I might, I still continue to be a failure at meditation. I have tried counting my breaths. I have tried focusing on relaxing images. I have tried the Jesus Prayer. The result is always the same only nowadays the focus might be more on the likes of the Boston Red Sox or Gillian Anderson. I do have some success while running—perhaps an unconventional method, but nonetheless it is the only way I've found to become quiet and inner-directed so that I can listen.

My experiences with retreats were more enjoyable. Typically, our class would be transported to a retreat center where we would focus on prayer and receive spiritual guidance from a visiting Jesuit. I would leave these experiences with the old mystical glow. Sadly, this glow would fade and for a time I became suspicious of retreats, seeing them as merely emotional highs with little lasting effect. Thankfully, this changed in 1986, as we will later see.

Another frustration of retreats was leaving with the resolve to avoid sin only to "fall" into it within days or even hours.

Reflection: What have your experiences been with retreats or other forms of withdrawal for the purpose of reflection?

This, then, is probably as appropriate a place as any to introduce that great paradoxical domain of agony and ecstasy. That paradox of mysticism and sensuality. In more ways than one, sex becomes an issue of great spiritual import for many of us.

For Catholics raised in the fifties and sixties, sex was largely approached with negativity. Masturbation, that oh-so-common great discovery of adolescence, was viewed as a terrible sin, worse than treason and possibly murder. As such, many of us, male and female alike, emerged into adolescence primed to view sex with a maddening combination of intense interest and deep guilt.

Edward Hays has written a beautiful book about what he terms "natural spirituality," describing it as, ". . . a return to that ageless friendship with creation that shows itself in a reverence for all nature" (*Pray All Ways.* Forest of Peace: Leavenworth KS, 1981, p. 16). Hays is responding to the dualism inherent in the above-mentioned attitude about sexuality. The attitude that spirit is better than flesh. That we are to "rise above" our base natures. Hays observes: "Whenever we reject our human nature (our bodies, sexuality, emotions), we also reject the God who created us as cosmic amphibians, as people intended to live in two worlds as one" (*ibid,* p. 16). He sums up the dilemma of many Catholics and Christians: "Today, we bear the wounds of hundreds of years of religious wars between the spirit and the flesh. Instead of tasting the fruit of communion between the two" (*op.cit,* p. 17). These are powerful words! They imply a theology of the body that does more than merely tolerate the flesh. They speak to a spirituality which points to God through the flesh, not in spite of the flesh.

Reflection: What impact did your early experiences with sex have on your emerging spirituality?

In the next chapter, we will explore the place of loving relationships on the spiritual path. But our sexuality emerges much sooner than our capacity to be present in intimate relationships. Some of these early sexual experiences have lasting impact on our psyche and our spirit.

The general religion of the body with which I grew up was the admiration of mortification. I would hear about or read about saints who would flog themselves, throw themselves into icy water, even starve themselves. I would feel guilty for craving a hamburger on Fridays, believing that somehow this was sinful self-indulgence. Like many of my generation, I grew up quite out of touch with my body. I remember when I was in high school hearing a line from the play *The Fantastiks:* "Celebrate sensation!" This was a notion that sounded almost sinful. Yet I also knew that I enjoyed the smell of burning leaves in autumn. I enjoyed the taste of fresh oranges, of chocolate. I loved music. I thought Jean Simmons in the film *Spartacus* was the most beautiful woman on earth. And when I danced with a girl, my skin would tingle. But it would be years before I could consider such delights to be a form of praise of the Almighty.

In a similar manner, there was much emphasis placed on sexual thoughts. In what constituted bad psychology, we were encouraged to avoid sexual thoughts. Good psychology would tell you that the more you try not to think about something, say, the feeling of your tongue in your mouth, the more you become aware of the very thing you're trying not to think about. So it is with sexual thoughts. The more we tried to avoid them , the stronger they became. Healthier thinking comes from this story retold by Joseph Telushkin: ". . . a man is reputed to have asked the eighteenth century Baal Shem Tov, the founder of Hasidism, how a person could discern a true religious leader from a false one. Baal Shem Tov answered, 'Ask him if he knows a way to prevent impure thoughts. If he says he does, he's a charlatan' " (*Jewish Wisdom.* William Morrow & Co., 1994, p. 132).

Sadly, some of us are sexually wounded early in life. Sexual abuse is far more common than we can imagine. The shame, fear, and anger carried by sexual abuse victims can sometimes haunt their adult years and have devastating impact on adult relationships. Some of these sexual wounds may also have spiritual components. I have heard more than a few victims of childhood sexual abuse wonder, "Why did God permit that?" Comments about choices made by adults rarely offer comfort. (Ironically, the one spiritual input that often *is* a comfort are the words of Jesus: "If anyone should harm these little ones, it would be better if he had a millstone tied about his neck and thrown into the water." The image of Jesus kicking butt was far more meaningful than any platitudes about forgiveness!)

Reflection: If early sexual trauma has been a part of your journey, reflect on how such trauma affected you spiritually.

The issue of sexual identity has been a source of struggle for some, including struggles at a spiritual level. Many religions have condemned and continue to condemn homosexuality. And not just homosexual behavior, but the condition of homosexuality. Therefore, as some have struggled to accept being gay, they have had to do so within the context of religious condemnation. Such wounds can run very deep. And yet, ironically, many of the clergy of my own Catholic Church, hardly a gay-friendly religion, are now gay.

Reflection: What was the impact of any sexual identity struggles on your spirituality? Did you experience any conflict/rejection within your religious tradition that related to being gay?

What, then, might constitute a healthy life-affirming theology of the body and of sexuality? First of all, take note from Edward Hays and consider that our bodies can be an effective and profound vehicle for connecting with and experiencing God. If mysticism is indeed a deep sensing of connectedness, then sexual expression provides a powerful and readily available vehicle for such mysticism.

We may also find help developing a healthy, responsible theology of sexuality from Buddhism. The Noble Eightfold Path of Buddhism includes Right Action. And according to Thich Nhat Hahn, Right Action, first of all, places our sexual behavior within the larger context of ". . . the practice of touching love and preventing harm, the practice of nonviolence toward ourselves and others" (*The Heart of the Buddha's Teachings.* Broadway Books: New York, 1998, p. 94). Right Action is closely connected to the Five Mindfulness Trainings. The Third Mindfulness Training is about sexuality:

> Aware of the suffering caused by sexual misconduct, I am committed to cultivating responsibility and learning ways to protect the safety and integrity of individuals, couples, families, and society. I am determined not to engage in sexual relations without love and long-term commitment. To preserve the happiness of myself and others, I am determined to respect my commitments and the commitments of others. I will do everything in my power to protect children from sexual abuse and to prevent couples and families from being broken by sexual misconduct.

When I reflect on this bit of Buddhist wisdom, I wonder what it would have been like to have had such thinking presented to me as a format for shaping my sexuality. Such positive, affirming thinking would, I suspect, have had a much different impact than did the dualistic, sin-based approach that most of us experienced.

Before moving on, I'd like to reflect for a moment on celibacy. It is a key element of the spiritual journeys of some whom I respect very much and was to an extent at the heart of my ultimate decision to not pursue priesthood. I have counseled many Catholic priests and sisters over the years and shared as best I could in their ongoing struggles with celibacy. What has become clear to me is that those who did not have a spiritual grounding for celibacy struggled more with it. In other words, some of those good people acknowledge viewing celibacy as one of the "terms of the contract" without having any spiritual perspective on it. In such cases, living a celibate life may become a case of teeth gritting and cold showers with no spiritual notions for support and comfort.

But is celibacy merely a neurotic "leftover" from less enlightened times? Or does it have some point, some spiritual virtue, that eludes us moderns? Kathleen Norris gives us pause with her reflections on the celibacy practiced at her beloved Benedictine community. She notes that the practice of celibacy frees these men and women to be present to one another in profound ways that can become obscured by the sexualizing of relationships. Norris writes:

> With someone who is practicing celibacy well, we may sense that we are being listened to in a refreshingly deep way. And this is the purpose of celibacy, not to attain some impossible cerebral goal but to make oneself available to others body *and* soul (*The Cloister Walk*. Riverhead: New York, 1996, p. 121).

This raises a powerful point for reflection, one that I find surprisingly relevant. In my work as a therapist, I am called to be present to clients in intimate, *nonsexual* ways. This does not mean that I deny any of my sexual feelings in response to a client. It means that I choose not to act on these feelings, in large part so that my client and I can explore more deeply others forms of intimacy which arise within the context of a nonsexual relationship. In this sense, celibacy in therapy is not merely one of the terms of the contract. The expression of our sexuality is an earthly delight that we set aside so that other types of intimacy may blossom more freely and deeply. (Granted, in my case, such celibacy comes more easily thanks to an intimate relationship at multiple levels with my wife of thirty-one years.)

Norris's thoughts help me understand the celibacy of those remarkable few—the Shakers. Of late, I've found myself drawn to the Shakers whose number continues to dwindle (as of this writing there are six left). They seem to have developed a ministry where tired souls come to their home at Sabathday Lake in Maine to spend some quiet time away from the mad world, absorbing the peacefulness which the Shaker way of life seems to convey. Such peacefulness and spiritual focus would be, I believe, difficult to come by if not for their celibate lifestyle.

By the end of my senior year, I'd begun to put on hold the idea of entering the seminary of the Holy Cross Fathers. Cold feet? Divine guidance?

Probably a little of both. A definite factor was my growing concern that I would struggle as a celibate. In any case, I elected to stay in town for college. I enrolled at the University of Scranton. The local Jesuit college.

Reflection: What have your experiences been with celibacy? How does it fit into your spiritual understandings of sex and sexuality?

CHAPTER 8

On Loving

The significant event of my freshman year in college occurred in the spring. I knew of the University Players, the school drama group with a reputation for cast parties. I was too shy to try out for their fall production, even though I had done some plays in high school. However, one March afternoon I noticed a sign announcing auditions for a spring production of *Spoon River Anthology,* a stage version of the poems of Edgar Lee Masters. I had read many of these poems in high school and truly loved them. This I could not pass up. When I came to auditions, the faculty director, a kind and gentle spirit named Bernard McGurl, greeted me warmly. He had judged me in a high school speech contest and was pleased to see me. I was cast and spent the next four years doing a variety of roles.

Art has played a major role in my spiritual journey. Directions, even answers, which my Catholicism did not provide, were uncovered through art. Thornton Wilder's *Our Town,* for example, has long been a rich source of meditative material. Consider these words, relevant to the topic at hand:

> You know how it is: you're twenty-one or twenty-two and you make some decisions; then whisssh! You're seventy; you've been a lawyer for fifty years and that white-haired lady at your side has eaten over fifty thousand meals with you. How do such things begin? (*Our Town.* Harper & Row: New York, 1968, p. 60).

Music has also enriched my path. Certain songs still have a way of bypassing my intellectualism and tapping into my feelings. Hymns such as "Be Not Afraid" and "You Are Near" have been a source of great comfort during times of trial. Some travelers clearly benefit from the visual arts. Henri Nouwen's biographer portrays Nouwen's work with various religious icons to enhance his journey. For me, standing before Dali's *The Last Supper* was a deep spiritual moment.

Reflection: What works of art have enriched your spiritual journey? How often do you allow yourself to make contact with these works?

The significance of theater was not the roles or the parties but the fact that, through theater, I met the young woman who was to become my wife.

Learning about loving has been a critical facet of my spiritual journey. Tending toward introversion, I have needed to be challenged to explore intimacy and vulnerability. My wife is an extrovert and at ease with her feelings. As such, our life together has not been dull.

Saint Paul says it clearly: "God is love, and he who abides in love abides in God and God in him." Yet we seem to think of spiritual journeys in individual terms. I would argue that one's history of and experience with loving intimate relationships is a key facet of the spiritual autobiography.

Reflection: As simple as it may sound, make a list of the people in your life whom you love and/or have loved.

What kind of love are we talking about here? Don't limit yourself by definitions. List whatever comes to you as loving, be it deep platonic love, head-over-heels puppy love, passionate love, parental love, or whatever form loving has taken in your life. All the loving you've experienced has been instructive on the spiritual path.

The topic of love has intrigued poets, philosophers, and psychologists for centuries and continues to be explored from multiple angles. As a guide, however, for assessing just how we are doing as far as being lovers is concerned, I find great help from the late Morton Kelsey.

Father Kelsey was a gentle man who wrote extensively on the interface of psychology and spirituality. Though I only met him once, I regard him as a spiritual mentor. In his book *Companions on the Inner Way: The Art of Spiritual Guidance* (Crossroad: New York, 1983), Father Kelsey explores what he sees as thirteen facets of human loving. I use his thoughts here to propose an inventory to be used for self-examination. Approach it not from a position of judgment but from a position of growth. We all, each and every one of us, saint or sinner, can stand to become even better lovers.

Reflection: Work on the following Inventory of Loving.

1. Have I made a conscious commitment to become a loving person? Is becoming a loving person even something I am interested in? Where does it fall on my list of priorities? If it is not my first priority, everything that comes before it will impact and limit my capacity to love. If, for example, money is my priority, then the pursuit of money may take precedence over the experience of love.

2. To what degree does my spiritual world reflect self-discipline? As Kelsey says, "Disciplined people are not subject to every whim, are not run by every unconscious motive and desire" (Kelsey, Morton, *Companions on the Inner Way: The Art of Spiritual Guidance,* Crossroad: New York, 1983, p. 200). It is ironic to consider that something as seemingly spontaneous as loving would require a degree of self-discipline, yet we also know that the acquisition of a certain trait or outcome, e.g., physical fitness, requires consistent repetition of a certain course of action (see Patterson, Richard B., *Becoming a Modern Contemplative: A Psychospiritual Model for Personal Growth.* Loyola University Press: Chicago, 1995).

3. How well do I love myself? This, I believe, is one of the great challenges of loving. Time and again I have counseled persons of service—therapists, priests and sisters, persons working in social justice, physicians. Without exception, these persons give freely of love and compassion yet judge themselves harshly. I remember counseling with a priest who faulted himself along certain lines. He sat berating himself and I asked him, "Tell me, when someone comes to you and confesses those sins, is this how you respond?" He was horrified, saying, "I would never say that to a penitent." So to assess myself as a lover, I need to examine how well I treat myself physically, mentally, emotionally, and spiritually. Do I treat my body gently or do I abuse it? Do I affirm myself or pass judgment? Do I place myself in needless stress or do I allow myself experiences that give me joy? Is my spirituality filled with fear or with celebration? (See also Patterson, Richard B., *Encounters with Angels: Psyche and Spirit in the Counseling Situation.* Loyola University Press: Chicago, 1992, chapter 8.)

4. How well do I listen? One of the finest gifts my daughter Becky ever gave me was in the midst of an argument. As I was berating her about something, she cried out in frustration, "Dad, you're not listening to me!" She was right. I became so focused on control and being right that I was shutting her out. As psychologist Carl Rogers (see, for example, *On Becoming a Person,* Mariner Books: New York, 1995) illustrated so beautifully, listening is not passive. We are involved. We express verbally and nonverbally that we are paying attention. We feed back what we are hearing to ensure accuracy. We do not interrupt. I recall one courageous woman who came to me years ago. She outlined her problem and I then proceeded to expostulate on her problem. Tactfully, she put up her hand and asked, "Would you be quiet and please just listen for a moment?"

5. How do I deal with my feelings of hurt? Withholding of negative feelings can give rise to resentments and/or acts of explosiveness and vengeance. Yet most of us hold on to such feelings, perhaps out of fear, perhaps out of payback. Sharing one's feelings of hurt is a risk. We make ourselves vulnerable to the person who hurt us. Thus, we need to evaluate the wisdom of sharing negative feelings based on the relationship's track record for dealing with them. In other words, even if this person hurt me, do I trust him/her?

6. How well do I do loving those closest to me? Many of us, especially in the helping and healing professions, pour out compassion to others but then treat our own loved ones poorly, taking out our frustrations on them or expecting special treatment because we spend such long hours being of service. To see how I am doing with loving, I need to look no further than my own family. How affirming and encouraging am I of them? How much and how often do I encourage the growth of each one? How available do I make myself? How much do I share?

7. How hospitable and welcoming am I to strangers? This does not mean that I should give money to every street person or invite him or her home for dinner. But it does means that I should not pass judgment on each street corner. Closer to home, there are constant opportunities to make others feel welcome. Do I introduce myself to the new neighbor? If I belong to a club or support group, do I greet each newcomer or do I hang back with those I know?

8. Finally, we come to the greatest challenge to loving—the love of one's enemies. Here we need to recall Kelsey's observation: ". . . my enemies are not only those whom I do not like but those who do not like me" (*op. cit.*, p. 207). It may be helpful to first make a list of your enemies. Can you look at each name and identify something about that person that you admire? Do you gossip or condone gossip about each person on your list? Which ones are targets of resentments?

One-to-one long-term relationships may be one of the most powerful schools in loving. For in long-term relationships, we experience all the challenges of tolerance and acceptance. We experience the temptation to take good relationships for granted, to not work on them constantly. Our "Shadow" side displays itself with alarming regularity.

Psychiatrist Carl Jung provided us with the great insight of the Shadow. This is a part of one's personality to which we do not like to admit. It is that within us which is potentially destructive. Our potential to violence, to selfishness, even to unbridled lust resides within our Shadow. The more we deny something within ourselves, the stronger it becomes within our Shadow.

But the effort to push the Shadow away does not work. It presses to be faced and integrated, a truly daunting task. It shows up when we least want it. And it especially shows up in our most intimate relationships, both as unpleasant, seemingly foreign modes of behavior and, more often, as projections. Maggie Scarf puts the Shadow Dance in this way: "Projections tend, generally speaking, to be *exchanges*—trades, so to speak, of denied parts, which both members of the couple have agreed to make. Then each one sees, in the partner, what cannot be perceived in the self—and struggles, ceaselessly, to change it" ("Meeting our opposites in husbands and wives," in Connie Zweig and Jeremiah Abrams' *Meeting the Shadow.* Jeremy Tarcher: New York, 1991, p. 72).

In college days, however, I was smitten—that head-over-heels-in-love rush that many of us spend a lifetime trying to recapture. I had little sense of what was going on.

Reflection: What experiences have you had with "falling in love"? How did they turn out?

CHAPTER 9

On Ethics

The Jesuits continued their work on my thinking abilities although in college I became much less focused on studies, discovering that I had some capacity to "fake it." Consequently, classes in English, languages, math, economics, and so on, came and went with little sticking. The only thing I remember from economics, for example, is "guns and butter." But a few classes stayed with me. One was history, a class taught by a man named Frank Brown. In any case, Mr. Brown was a performer, a man who did more than teach history. He *enacted it!* His style would shape my own efforts at teaching in future years.

Of even greater impact were the ethics classes taught by Father Bernard Suppe. Father Suppe was an intense man who challenged us to have our own opinions about ethical matters and be prepared to defend them. I attended Father Suppe's classes in 1969 and 1970, intense years for both my church and my country.

My church was feeling the initial strains that eventually caused it to almost tear apart. The focus of this strain was birth control. Father Suppe exposed us to both sides of the argument. We studied what was the majority opinion in favor of birth control as well as Pope Paul VI's stand against it. Again, we were encouraged to *think.*

These years also marked another of my ever more frequent experiences of inner contradictions. I grew increasingly disenchanted with our country's involvement in Vietnam and even participated in marches. But at the same time I was enrolled in ROTC, which meant that, upon graduation, I would be commissioned as an officer in the U.S. Army. Friends took a position of nonviolence and therefore became conscientious objectors. I looked at my history of numerous fistfights and concluded that I was a violent person and therefore could not in good conscience be an objector. I was indeed thinking for myself, albeit from a flawed perspective of nonviolence. Only later would I realize that the very inner violence which I felt blocked me was actually the key to a nonviolent stance. This realization, however, came after four years of service in the army.

So, thanks to Father Suppe, I wrestled with two major ethical issues—birth control and nonviolence—and came to my own conclusions. This was an early experience of genuine spiritual power.

Reflection: What were some of your notable ethical struggles as a young adult? How did you resolve them?

One potent aspect of my spiritual journey, then, has been to discern what I really believed about right and wrong, even if such beliefs stood in contradiction to the tenets of the Church. I was exposed to the concepts of situational ethics, which posited the criterion of love as a basis for ethical belief and not the authority of the Church. In any given situation, what appeared to be the most loving course of action? It was during this time that I was challenged to truly examine what I believed and why.

In time I would recognize a need to "sin bravely." In other words, I would see that some actions which I'd been taught were sinful probably weren't, and some actions which were not discussed or strongly emphasized probably were. Thus, I concluded that masturbation, for example, was not a big deal, while calling someone a "faggot" or "nigger" was.

Reflection: How has your understanding of right and wrong changed over time?

One other Jesuit who enriched my journey was Father John Long. Already retired when I met him, Father Long had been the president of the university and had guided it through a time of great growth. He had an aura of great peacefulness, even holiness. He accompanied our college Sodality on a retreat, and I recall especially one evening when we all sat informally with him as he talked about the spiritual life. One of the things he spoke of was the afterlife. "I don't believe much in fire and brimstone," he said. "I believe hell involves complete preoccupation with self. As if you are floating in a vacuum, orbiting your self and nothing else." Father Long was, I believe, one of a handful of saints I have been privileged to meet along the way.

Some people apparently have a problem with the Catholic notion of saints, believing that it is wrong to pray to one of these personages. Regardless, I believe that saints are persons of great character held up to us as examples. If there is an afterlife, these people may have an inside track.

I have met other saintly people over the years, some in the counseling room. They were not "perfect" people. Rather, they strove to lead a good life, treated others well, tried to grow spiritually, and handled painful situations with a great degree of heroism. My list of saints probably reveals what I actually believe about goodness.

On the other hand, I have met people over the years whom I can only describe as embodying evil. While I try to avoid judging others, I nonetheless find some unpleasant or annoying. But these are not the ones I am talking about. I am talking about the man who, after learning he'd blinded his infant daughter with a beating, shrugged his shoulders and said, "Oh well . . ." Or the man who smugly told the wife he'd beaten many times that she deserved what she'd received. These persons perpetrate harmful acts without any sense of remorse.

Reflection: Make a list of saintly people you've encountered (even if a belief in saints is not part of your path). What did you learn from them? In the same manner, make a list of people you've met who seemed to project evil. What impact did they have on you?

Finally, my college years were marked by my initial exposure to psychology, to what would become my vocational path. I first majored in sociology and intended to be a social worker. (I'd been inspired by actor George C. Scott in the television series *East Side, West Side.*) Then I discovered that social workers made little money—my intentions were not completely noble—and so I switched to psychology.

I can say with certainty that I knew *nothing* about psychology. I suppose I'd heard the name Freud somewhere and had a vague memory of being bored by a movie about him. I'd never heard of B.F. Skinner.

Psychology gradually opened up to me a different way of thinking about myself and those around me. How had the deaths of my sisters affected me, my brother, and my parents? What kind of relationship did I have with each of my parents and how did that affect who I was? These and other questions simply had never occurred to me, in part because, to this point, things had been answered through religion.

B. F. Skinner, however, presented a challenge. His theory was strictly mechanistic. We learned Skinnerian psychology by training rats to do things such as play basketball (actually a neat trick!). This, Skinner said, was the same way we humans learned. Skinner was brilliant and compelling. But the man/woman he articulated was quite different from the spiritual being I was more familiar with. If Skinner was right, where, if anywhere, does God fit in? Thus, the seeds of a developing inner debate were sown. Secular psychology versus Catholicism. It would be years before I found any common ground.

In my senior year I became engaged and was also accepted into Indiana University's graduate school in a program, it turned out, that had once been headed by Skinner. It was also a *public* university, not a private Catholic school. The kind of school I'd been warned about when I was young. ("If you go to one of those public colleges, you'll be turned into an *atheist!*")

Reflection: Have you confronted a system of ideas that challenged the foundation of your spiritual beliefs?

CHAPTER 10

On Healing Relationships

When I entered graduate school at Indiana University, I was drinking on a daily basis and continued for the next thirteen years. My spiritual world was somewhat colored by the impact of addiction. So, despite the inroads made by the Jesuits, there were areas of growth and development as well as areas of extreme dead weight. Old *Baltimore Catechism* views still had their hold on me. "Old tapes," as they say.

Old tapes are those spiritual beliefs which at a conscious level we may seriously question but at the unconscious level they continue to generate guilt and fear. For example. I had long questioned the notion that you *had* to worship God on a given day, especially when Saturday evening masses were added and *counted* for Sunday. "If Saturday's OK, then why not Thursday?" I would reason. But the old tapes would argue, "Ah, but suppose you're wrong. Then you'll be in big trouble on Judgment Day!" And so the guilt would win out.

I nearly flunked out of graduate school the first year, thanks in part to alcohol. But the department put me on academic probation and kept me around. The second year held two significant events which greatly impacted my spiritual journey—my discovery of the enterprise of psychotherapy and the birth of my son.

That year marked the beginnings of actual psychotherapy with honest-to-God clients. I took an initial psychotherapy course, eagerly looking forward to exploring various approaches to therapy. Unfortunately, it quickly became apparent that the course would explore research, not practice. So, I designed a reading program of my own through which I read and read and read various theories of therapy. I read Carl Rogers and Albert Ellis, Sigmund Freud, and Karl Jung, Fritz Perls, and, especially, Viktor Frankl.

Through Rogers, I learned the importance of approaching others with an attitude of respect and acceptance. I learned the value of not judging others.

I did not like confrontation and had much trouble with anger, so Rogers' warm, accepting approach suited my personality well.

Rogers also helped me grasp the importance of listening. It is so tempting, when dealing with others in pain, to be quick with the pat answer, the "obvious" solution. Rogers clearly conveyed the power of listening and further conveyed that listening is not necessarily passive. I have since seen that, while I may always hear, I don't always listen. And so I learned to listen well, but in the process I forgot, or perhaps never learned, that most important spiritual listening—I didn't listen to God.

Most of my praying is talking *at* God. A list of demands. A litany of worries. The words of Samuel—"Speak, Lord. Your servant is listening"—eluded me. I still struggle mightily with becoming quiet and simply sitting and waiting. For what? For the words of God. For when I do manage to quiet the flow of words, sometimes I hear another Voice. Very quiet, and from very deep inside. Jesus said, "The Kingdom of God is within you," but I have come to understand that, to hear the words of that Kingdom, I must listen. And I rarely do that well.

Reflection: In what ways do you listen to God?

There have been times over the years when I have managed to quiet myself and listen for the Voice of God and hear—nothing! God is silent! It would seem that, at times, God withdraws. Henri Nouwen articulates this Taoist notion in relationship to Jesus: "If we deny the pain of his absence we will not be able to taste his sustaining presence. . . ." (*Seeds of Hope: A Henri Nouwen Reader.* Robert Durback, ed. Image Books: New York, 1997, p. 130).

Reflection: In what ways have you experienced God's absence?

But then I read Viktor Frankl. Although I didn't realize it at the time, Frankl's work was the first key link in the bridge to establish a connection between the spiritual and psychological domains. Viktor Frankl was a Jewish psychiatrist who suffered at the hands of Hitler's Third Reich. From his experiences evolved his theory of logotherapy in which he examined the issue of *meaning* in a person's life. In fact, Frankl expanded on a line of thought developed by Freud and Adler, suggesting that we are endowed with an inherent desire to find meaning. He referred to this as "the will to meaning."

Frankl's theories have stayed with me since 1972 when I first encountered his work. His theory of the will to meaning has been of value in my counseling and has also been an important signpost in my own spiritual journey.

Frankl, among other things, suggested, obviously from firsthand experience, that suffering could have meaning, and that finding meaning in suffering made it bearable. Clearly, given my life experiences, I was drawn to such a line of thought. I have conversed with many courageous persons struggling to find meaning in their suffering. A parent who has lost a child. A person facing the terminal stages of AIDS. A victim of brutal childhood sexual abuse. The notion of finding meaning in such suffering has been a powerful beacon.

Reflection: What are/have been themes of meaning in your journey so far? Have you ever struggled with feeling that your life had become devoid of meaning?

During my second year, I began experiencing others' suffering through the vehicle of psychotherapy. I still vividly remember many of those early clients. How patient they were! How much they taught me! So it would be in the years ahead. Many who came to me for help would end up teaching me in ways they never knew. Some of their stories will be found in the pages ahead.

Through psychotherapy, I was exposed to yet another type of relationship—doctor/patient. Even though it was my job to listen and perhaps to help, I quickly discovered that, like the other relationships in my life, this one could be a source for my own growth and would challenge me to confront blind spots.

Reflection: What are/have been themes of meaning in your journey so far? Have you ever struggled with feeling that your life had become devoid of meaning?

Quotes

Meditation books have become quite popular in recovery circles. These books often include quotes that have some meaning to the author/editor. It has occurred to me that each of us may have such a book within us consisting of quotes and words which have stayed with us, providing hope, guidance, a good laugh, or a reminder of an insight. I want to share a few of my own favorite quotes with you, mainly to encourage you to include your own collection of favorite quotes in our spiritual autobiography. Many of mine occur throughout this book. In no particular order, here are a few more:

". . . people chosen to be messengers of the most High rarely even know they are His messengers" (Lawrence Kushner, *Honey from the Rock.* Jewish Lights: Woodstock, VT, 1991).

"What we lack is not a will to believe but a will to wonder" (Abraham Joshua Heschel, *Man is Not Alone.* Noonday Press, 1997).

"As long as we're here, we might as well play." (Ram Dass and Paul Gorman, *How Can I Help? Stories and Reflections on Service.* Knopf: New York, 1985).

"You may or may not find the answer by demanding to know, but you will surely never find the answer by fearing to ask" (William Safire, *The First Dissident.* Random House: New York, 1993).

Reflection: Use this space simply to collect some of your favorite quotes.

CHAPTER 11

On Parenting

During my second year of graduate school, our first child, Matthew Dismas, was born. Thus began my journey of fatherhood, certainly one of the most maddening, meaningful, and humbling stretches of road on my spiritual passage.

Matthew was an immediate source of one gift. With him present in our very tiny apartment, I cut back on smoking and, within ten days of his birth, quit completely, thereby overcoming one of my addictions.

In the next four years were be blessed with three more children, the last two being twins. Early on, in dialogue with my wife, I faced the decision of what I wanted my children to think about religion in general and Catholicism in particular. Is it a surprise that one point I emphasized is that they *think* about what they believe? And as adults this is how each of them approaches spiritual matters. While I don't always agree with choices they have made, I am appreciative that they have thought through spiritual decisions.

Through my children's struggles, I have seen more clearly some of the failings of my own Catholicism. For my children, rituals have often been a source of boredom. In Catholic schools, they experienced the undercurrents of racism. It appears that Catholicism does not offer them what they seek. They have all looked elsewhere and in some ways have found some answers that work better for them.

In many ways, too, parenting exposed me to my own issues with control. For years, I had a recurring dream. One of my children would be doing something that put them in danger. I would be beside myself with rage, yelling and trying to get them out of danger. I would feel badly about these dreams, thinking that they suggested an abusive side to my parenting. Then I realized that what fueled my rage was fear and that, out of fear, I would attempt to control. With this insight, the dreams ended. Often out of fear, we attempt to control our children's lives.

Yet I was also a believer in discipline. So parenting became a challenge of finding balance. Maintaining authority while always in the process of letting go. Holding on and letting go. Another spiritual theme was taking form.

Reflection: If you have children, how has your spiritual journey been affected by being a parent? By your children's spiritual journeys? What have you learned about controlling and letting go?

As I grappled with parenting, I would of course reflect on the parenting I'd received. I identified areas in which I wanted to parent like my dad and ways in which I wanted to be different. These reflections made me more aware of some ways in which I actually felt wounded. For example, when I was twelve years old, I stopped kissing my dad. "Men shake hands," I was told. I changed this, both in my relationships with my children and in my relationship with my dad. Throughout the rest of his life, I'd greet my dad with a kiss. He always responded.

My children also helped me hold onto the capacity for play. This may seem unrelated to spirituality, but I believe it is central. Play allows us to be silly, to let go, not to be caught up in appearances. It is the training ground for our creativity, a central spiritual quality. One of the nicest compliments I was paid as a therapist came from a charming four-year-old who told her mother I was "rather silly."

Some of us never really learned to play. The environment in which we were raised was too serious or perhaps simply without nurturance. Or we once knew how to play but, through the business of becoming an adult, we somehow forgot. What a great and tragic loss!

Reflection: What role has playing had in your spiritual growth?

While I was in the army, children and I discovered camping. This might seem trivial, but in fact the time I spent with my children in the presence of nature opened up another domain through which I could find connection to God. Nature, too, became integral to my children's spiritual journeys. For me, I rediscovered the mystical domain that I thought I'd lost. I found it in the forest.

Reflection: Has nature played any role in your spiritual journey?

There is, of course, a long tradition of God discovered through nature. Many of my spiritual mentors—Annie Dillard and Loren Eisley to name two—speak poetically of the spiritual domain experienced through the worlds of animals and plants and trees. Another favorite writer Terry Tempest Williams says it succinctly: "Wilderness courts our soul" (*Refuge: An Unnatural History of Family and Place.* Vintage: New York, 1991, p. 148).

The wonder of a child in the presence of nature opened my mind and heart. My children would be excited over an unexpected animal, be it a deer on a trail or an errant skunk wandering into a tent. They would eagerly seek out the first star. They would become quiet and reflective in the presence of a crackling campfire. They would exhibit a primitive fear we all share in the presence of night and the unknown. Thus, my children and the animals we encountered enriched my path.

Reflection: How has childhood wonder enriched your spiritual path?

One final spiritual encounter of some importance occurred during my Indiana days. We often had guest speakers at the clinic, and I invited a priest from the local campus Catholic Church. His name was Father John Shoettelkotte. During Father John's presentation, I asked how he helped persons who'd been wounded while attending Catholic schools. In a very disarming, nonjudgmental way, he said, "Well, I'd wonder why that person was blaming his spiritual struggles on some well-meaning old woman from twenty years ago." Well!

Father John's words obviously bothered me, in part because they were on target. I indeed had invested much energy in resentment toward the sisters and was thereby trying to avoid grappling with what I actually believed. Slowly, slowly, I began to let go of blaming the good sisters.

Reflection: Have you blamed any of your spiritual struggles on others? Write about it.

CHAPTER 12

Wounded Healer

After completing my studies at Indiana, we headed to Columbia, South Carolina, for a one-year internship. During that year of excellent training, I confronted some extremes of human suffering. I heard stories of unimaginable abuse. I felt utter helplessness in the presence of a severely suicidal sixteen-year-old who refused to talk. I felt a full range of emotions in response to my clients—from annoyance and dislike to sexual attraction.

Early in the year my fellow interns and I decided we'd like the opportunity for personal growth. We were referred to a man named Racine Brown who, for the better part of the year, provided us with an hour's worth of group therapy a week. This pivotal experience brought a realization that would stay with me and would prove central to my therapeutic approach—that I too was wounded. I became aware through this therapy that there was an emotional distance between my father and me. I became aware that I had much anger inside but was afraid to approach it. I stumbled over all sorts of impediments which impacted on my capacity to love.

It would still be a few years before I came across the notion of the "wounded healer" but I did realize that I would connect best with these wounded people by being more aware of what was within me—the angry teenager, the spiritual bankruptcy, even the craziness.

My wounds, too, became critical elements of my spiritual journey for, through my wounds, I came to see that, even in the midst of darkness and despair, healing is possible, and that the source of this healing is much more powerful than I.

Reflection: What do you consider to be your major wounds? What have your experiences been with the healing of those wounds? What has been the impact on your spiritual journey?

I also found myself wrestling with clients' problems which were frankly spiritual in nature. The aforementioned teenager had suffered a great deal of abuse in the name of religion. One man believed he was condemned to hell because he had the very normal tendency to have sexual thoughts about women other than his wife. In those days (and today) there was a tendency within the mental health professions to refer spiritual matters to chaplains for addressing. With support from my supervisors, I approached some of these issues directly, thereby learning that we are whole persons with a spiritual side that cannot be ignored or fragmented.

From South Carolina, we moved to Texas, where I began service in the United States Army. I spent my first year working on Fort Bliss, then moved to William Beaumont Hospital. I was still drinking a lot of beer on a daily basis. But two people came into my life who would play roles at a later time. I worked with Loyd G., and through him I met Jan W. Both became good friends. They also gave me exposure to the benefits of Alcoholics Anonymous, of which they were members. They both seemed to have a grasp on some spiritual truth that continued to elude me. And both clearly were wounded healers.

In some ways, though, my army years were also a spiritual desert. Outside of forays into the forest, I rarely had a sense of God's presence. I was going through the motions, showing up for Mass each Sunday.

Reflection: When have you had desert experiences where your spiritual world seemed barren and dry?

I n retrospect, this barrenness, as well as growing anxiety over what I would do when my tour of duty was up, led me to seek out a therapist. I'd done some reading of the psychology of Carl Jung and was drawn to his openness to spiritual experience. Further, a friend was seeing a therapist who happened to have some training in Jungian psychology, and spoke very highly of him. And so I undertook my first course of individual therapy was with a very gifted man, Ramon Lopes-Reyes.

Ramon was an older man who met clients in his home. My time with him, about six months' worth, was very productive and also humbling. Ramon quickly recognized that I wanted spiritual and psychological payoffs for which I was not ready and which I had not really earned. One dream dramatized my attitude:

> *I am traveling to the center of the earth. But rather than traveling through caves and trails, I am taking an elevator. When I get there, I do not find the Philosopher's Stone, but instead a hot dog—with thorns in it!*

I should offer some background to this dream. One evening, while I was administrative officer of the day at the hospital, I was reading Jung's *Man and His Symbols,* which included many stories with "Big Dreams" in them. By Big Dream, I mean a dream pregnant with deep meaning. I went to bed that night hoping I'd have a Big Dream. My hot dog dream was the result.

I did not like Ramon's ideas on the dream. For it seemed to be saying that I wanted deep spiritual payoffs but without paying the price. Over time I came to see the accuracy of this interpretation and realized some years later that I'd been granted my request. I'd been given a Big Dream. Be careful what you pray for!

Reflection: Have your dreams played a role in your spiritual journey? If so, how? Have you had any Big Dreams along the way? Write them down if you haven't already.

Reflection: What kind of "shortcuts" have you taken spiritually?

Ramon made one other point which had unseen impact. While exploring with me the state of my Catholicism, he commented almost in passing that, at some point in our adult life, we needed to grow up spiritually. This comment echoed Father John's comment from my Indiana days. Mired as I was in old tapes and addiction, I didn't really appreciate this comment at the time. But it stayed with me.

One other important development occurred while I was in the army. I discovered a form of meditation which worked for me. I took up running!

I found in time that running provided an inner-directed experience which allowed me to become reflective without distraction. Since those first runs on Fort Bliss, I have covered many miles and have not missed a day of running in over thirteen years. I do most of my praying while running. I am able to pause and reflect on that which impacts my life. Most of my creative inspirations have occurred while running. As strange as it may seem, running has played a key role in my spiritual journey. Saint Paul said, "I have finished the race. I have kept the faith." I may not have finished the race just yet, but running is clearly helping me keep the faith!

Reflection: Have you found a form of meditation that works for you? Describe it.

CHAPTER 13

Bridges from Psyche to Spirit

I left the army in 1979, choosing to open a private practice in the Southwest desert. My Catholic faith was in a pretty shabby state but I was once again motivated to take a course in self-study. I began to read about other religions and found myself especially drawn to Zen Buddhism. Perhaps it was the antiintellectual flavor of Zen that called to me. In any case, I read books that had a powerful impact. In particular, *Zen Mind, Beginner's Mind* by S. Suzuki (Weatherhill, 1997) and *Zen and the Art of Motorcycle Maintenance* by Robert Pirsig (Bantam Books, 1984) seemed to speak to me. Early on, I had an affirming dream. I was running with Salvador Minuchin, a famous family therapist whom I admired. Minuchin turned to me in the dream and said, "You're on the right track with your interest in Zen."

I'd grown up with the concept of the "One True Religion." Of course, many other religions view themselves as the O.T.R. In any case, this belief in the O.T.R. included a suspiciousness of other faiths. Dialogue with clients of various faiths had begun to erode this notion.

My son Andy, philosopher that he is, once suggested that religions were simply different opinions. Are they simply a waste of time? I believe that it is arrogant to ignore the teachings of other spiritual travelers. My own stumbling journey has been greatly enriched by Zen, by Judaism and Jewish mysticism. I resonated to the words of Rabbi Laurence Kushner: "Each person has a Torah, unique to that person, his or her innermost teaching. Some seem to know their Torah very early in life and speak and sing them in a myriad of ways. Others spend their whole lives stammering, shaping, and rehearsing them. Some are long, some short. Some are intricate and poetic, others are only a few words, and still others can only be spoken through gesture and example. But every soul has a Torah" (*God Was in This Place and I, I Did Not Know It.* Jewish Lights: Woodstock, VT, p. 177).

Reflection: If you were raised in a religious tradition, what facets have you held onto? How has your walk been enriched by other approaches to the spiritual journey?

At the time I was drawn to Zen, I cannot say that I knew for sure what was drawing me. I can say in retrospect that Buddhism has much to say about suffering, which was one of my central struggles. I can also say that, in the midst of addiction, I needed to begin thinking about attachments and letting go. Zen Buddhism seemed to provide something I needed without my knowing that I needed it. These experiences provided me with a beginning understanding of the idea of grace.

Reflection: As you reflect on your journey, do you see any points where you were provided with something you needed, even though you might not have known it at the time?

I suppose that I was ironically drawn to the somewhat antiintellectual flavor of Zen Buddhism. Zen seemed to encourage me to "let go" of my great need to understand something. In its own way, Zen seemed to suggest that, the more I felt I understood something spiritual, the further away I was from the truth. In Zen terms, "He who says does not know. He who knows does not say." Thus, Zen provided needed balance to what the Jesuits taught me about thinking.

Zen also helped me appreciate the paradoxical side of God. In the Gospels, Jesus often spoke in paradoxical terms ("The first shall be last and the last shall be first," for example). Zen provided a rich appreciation of paradox. Also enriching was the Buddhist notion of the Five Wonderful Precepts—"reverence for life, generosity, responsible sexual behavior, speaking and listening deeply, and ingesting only wholesome substances" (Hahn, *ibid,* p. 91).

During this time I also was exposed to Taoism. The Taoist notion of complementary polarities (Yin-Yang) also held powerful appeal. It helped me see that virtue, for example, was meaningless without my appreciation of sin. That light only made sense in relation to darkness. This greatly impacted my moral thinking. Several interpreters of Taoism pointed out that God might only have meaning in relation to not-God. And in true Taoist manner, Carl Jung spoke of God's Dark Side.

I continued to struggle with trying to find some sort of bridge which could encompass both my psychological background and my spiritual yearnings. I consulted with the local Catholic diocesan marriage tribunal, run by Joe Nelen, a gentle-spirited, brilliant priest. Over lunch one day, I shared my yearnings and Joe mentioned two writers to me—John A. Sanford and Morton Kelsey. I immediately went to a local bookstore and found a copy of John Sanford's *The Kingdom Within* (Harper-SanFrancisco, 1987). I also came across Henri Nouwen's *The Wounded Healer* (Image Books, 1979) and picked up a copy of Morton Kelsey's *Companions on the Inner Way* (Crossroad, 1983). A new world opened up to me!

Slowly, the bridge took form. Sanford's *The Kingdom Within* approaches the Gospels from the perspective of Jungian psychiatry and suggests that Jesus' parables have an inner meaning and relevance to the psychological journeys and struggles of each one of us. Sanford is not attempting to psychologize Jesus. Rather, he is exploring one particular approach to tapping the richness of Jesus' sayings. In particular, he opens up the Jungian approach to dreams as a tool for understanding Jesus' sayings.

I had studied dreams previously when I was seeing Ramon. But the works of Sanford spoke powerfully to the value of dreams on the spiritual path. I have tried to listen to my dreams since then. Often they are puzzling and obtuse. Sometimes they are disturbing. But if I take the time to listen, they can be a powerful guide on the journey.

A brief example. Somewhere during this time, I had a dream wherein I confronted an SS officer who was in some way jeopardizing some children. I drove him away and even pardoned him as he was leaving.

After waking from this dream, I felt rather heroic! But later it occurred to me that the SS officer was also a reflection of myself. Now I didn't feel quite so heroic.

The Jungian theory, however, suggested that this dream was trying, through the figure of the SS officer, to point me toward some aspect of my shadow side with which I needed to make contact. After some reflection, it occurred to me that the SS officer might represent self-discipline, a quality I sorely lack. Sadly, he represents more than that—my own capacity for cruelty among other things. But he did help me find some capacity for self-discipline, which in turn has made it possible for me to write.

But it was Nouwen's image of the "wounded healer" that truly haunted me. Nouwen, I would learn, did not create the image. It is an image that can be found in numerous cultures and is at the heart of shamanic religions practice. But Nouwen put the image in terms I could grasp.

A wounded healer is one who has suffered and been wounded but has faced his/her wounds, done some healing, and then draws upon those wounds as a resource for bringing healing to others. It is also an image which lies at the root of the current self-help movement. I felt drawn to it yet had limited insight into the core of my own woundedness.

Nouwen challenges us to embrace our own wounds as a resource to truly connect with others. Often we shrink from our own pain, wanting to find comfort without feeling the pain. As Jung said, "When we must deal with problems, we instinctively refuse to try the way that leads through darkness and obscurity. We wish to hear only of unequivocal results and completely forget that these results can only be brought about when we have ventured into and emerged again from the darkness" ("The Stages of Life" in *Modern Man in Search of a Soul.* Harvest Books: Orlando, FL, 1955, p. 97). Such avoidance has a great price tag. It becomes very difficult for us to be truly empathic, to genuinely feel one another's pain. And it becomes virtually impossible to grow.

I would like to claim that the first time I read Nouwen's *The Wounded Healer,* the clouds parted and I saw the light. But this wouldn't be true. The book struck a chord, but I didn't fully answer. In retrospect, I am reminded of the story of the preacher and the flood. The floodwaters were rising and a truck came along to take the preacher to high ground, but he refused, saying, "My prayers will save me." Then a boat came along as the waters continued to rise but again he turned them down, professing, "My prayers will save me!" Finally, a helicopter offered to pick him off of his rooftop. But again he refused. And he drowned. Needless to say, when he met his Lord, he was a bit upset. But the Lord said, "Well, I sent you help three times and you turned me down each time!"

So I was still insisting that I could fix my own messes without any help.

Reflection: Have there been points in your journey when help crossed your path but you turned it down?

CHAPTER 14

On Addiction

Thich Nhat Hanh tells a story about a man walking along a road (*Being Peace.* Parallex Press: Berkeley, CA, p. 65). Suddenly, another man comes racing by on a galloping horse. The first man calls out, "Where are you going in such a hurry?" and the second man shouts back, "I don't know. Ask the horse!" Many of us have had such horses in our lives, taking us to parts unknown with us having little control over the ride. For some of us, our horse was named "Alcohol." There are, however, many different horses. They represent our attachments and, in extreme, our addictions. Some people are driven by the horse of "Work and Success," others by a particular relationship. When our attachments become obsessive, then we are addicted, be it to a drug, a person, an activity. Our lives become organized around the attachment and the addiction.

One of the many brilliant insights of the founders of Alcoholics Anonymous was the spiritual nature of addiction, an insight that had some roots in the thoughts of Carl Jung. If we make something the priority of our lives, do we not substitute this entity, be it booze or money or fame or sex, for our god? We organize our lives around it, we long for it, we become fearful in its absence. When we become attached or addicted, we lose spiritual power.

Reflection: What "horses" have there been in your life? What "horses" are there now?

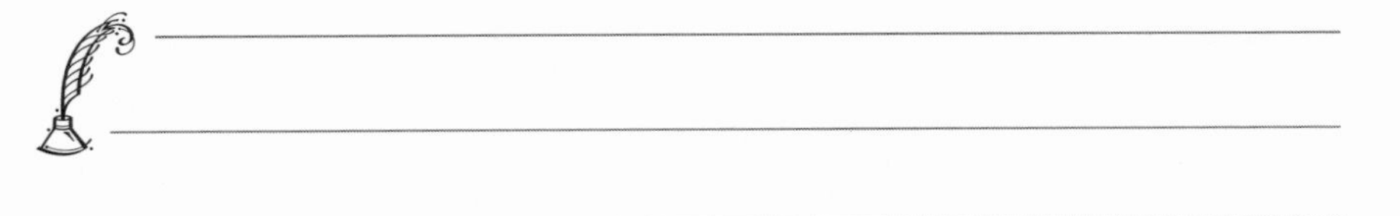

By 1983, I had been drinking daily for at least fifteen years. I was a beer drinker who gave up beer every Lent. Of course, during Lent I would switch to wine coolers, gin and tonics, and so forth. When I was in the army, we would often go to a nearby restaurant for lunch and I would have several beers. During Lent I'd switch to wine coolers, so whenever I went in there and ordered a wine cooler, our usual waitress would say, "Oh, it must be Lent!"

By mid 1983, I had read Henri Nouwen's *The Wounded Healer* twice, each time reflecting on ways in which I was wounded and each time pausing when I would consider my drinking. In May of 1983 I also read *He* by Robert Johnson. While considering the myth of the Fisher King, Johnson too reflected on woundedness. Again my thoughts touched on, then ran from, my drinking. In late May I went to a workshop conducted by my friend Gerald (Jerry) Bryan. At one point, Jerry suggested an imagery exercise that would focus on a wound. The word "Alcohol" popped into my head, but I moved on to something else.

Finally, on June 1, I went to see the film *Return of the Jedi.* My children grew up on the *Star Wars* trilogy and I too was entranced by it. I had begun to see a theme of woundedness developing. In *The Empire Strikes Back,* hero Luke Skywalker loses his hand in a battle with his father Darth Vader. This,

I felt, represented Luke's woundedness. I was anxious to see how this theme would develop in the third installment. Little did I know what I was in for.

Return of the Jedi is a story about redemption. Luke decides that his father Darth Vader has good in him and attempts to save him. However, the evil emperor provokes Luke instead to attack his father. In the process, Luke cuts off his father's hand. In a moment of spiritual awakening, Luke realizes that he and his father are connected in their woundedness. Ultimately he rescues his father, helping Darth Vader reclaim his own goodness.

As I watched this film, something deep stirred within me. The themes of woundedness and redemption moved me. I would like to tell you that I did not drink after that movie, but I did. True to form, that night I drank. But the next morning I awoke with the thought that it was time for me to face my drinking.

I would like to take credit for that moment, but I can't. It did not come from me. It came from somewhere else. That moment, on the morning of June 2, 1983, is the clearest understanding I have had or perhaps ever will have of God's grace.

A good friend, Sister Alice Holden, once suggested to me that grace is the experience of God sharing his/her power. (I also appreciate Alice as one of the women who helped me experience the feminine side of God.) This was my experience that moment. I felt I'd been given a level of power that had not touched me before. In time I saw that the grace had not been confined to that morning. It was present in Nouwen's and Johnson's books and in Jerry Bryan's workshop. It was present in *Return of the Jedi.*

Reflection: Describe an experience of grace that you understand was a taste of God's power for you.

I am a stubborn person and so, even with this gift of grace, my arrogance inclined me to want to sober up on my own. So for the next ten days I "white-knuckled" it (i.e., tried not to drink through sheer willpower). I mentioned earlier a man named Loyd G. Loyd had left El Paso for an assignment in Hawaii; however, shortly before June 2, 1983, he returned to El Paso. As it happened, on my ninth day of sobriety, I had lunch with Loyd. When he dropped me off at my office, I mentioned, "Loyd, I'm trying to do something about my drinking." Loyd burst into tears and said, "God, Rich. That's an answer to a prayer!" He had seen and known and was waiting for me. So later that day I called Loyd and asked him to take me to an Alcoholics Anonymous meeting.

Such was my journey to the doors of AA. Help had been sent my way many times, only to be turned down. Thankfully, though, I reached out before drowning.

When I sat down next to a lady in that first meeting, I realized she had been a client of mine. She stared at me and said, "You're . . ." and I nodded. "Are you one of us?" she asked. All I could say was that I was there to find out. On the way back to my office, I almost was involved in three different car accidents! About a week later, I walked into the AA club and was met by my friend Jan W., who hugged me without a word. I had the sense she'd also been waiting for me.

In time I came to know the steps and traditions of AA. I did my best to walk those steps. I witnessed many people come and stay and just as many come and go. Most especially, I came to a new understanding of spirituality and faith.

The founders of AA articulated that the path to recovery from addiction is fundamentally spiritual in nature. The founders stated it directly: "As soon as we admitted the possible existence of a Creative Intelligence, a Spirit of the Universe underlying the totality of things, we began to be possessed of a new sense of power and direction. . ." (*Alcoholics Anonymous.* Third Edition. Alcoholics Anonymous: New York, 1976, p. 46). It is an insight summarized well by Carl Jung in a letter to one of AA's cofounders. In writing about an alcoholic known to both of them, Jung wrote: "His craving for alcohol was the equivalent, on a low level, of the spiritual thirst of our being for wholeness, expressed in medieval language: the union with God" (W., Bill, *The Language of the Heart: Bill W's Grapevine Writings.* AA Grapevine Inc.: New York, 1988, p. 280).

In addiction, then, we are searching for something. This in many ways proves to be the case at a more human level as well. Why did I drink? To fit in. To relax. To set my troubles aside. To feel better about myself. These are valid and valuable goals. The problem is with the means to these goals.

Facets of addiction are reflected in terms such as obsession, compulsion, and attachment. In essence, an addiction is a horse as mentioned earlier, some behavioral pattern that runs our lives against our values and our better judgment.

Anne Wilson Schaef indicates two types of addictions (*When Society Becomes an Addict.* Harper & Row: San Francisco, 1987, p. 20 ff): substance and process. Substances include food, drugs, and alcohol while process addictions can include work, gambling, sex, etc. The point here is to understand the spiritual component of addiction. In essence, the booze, the sex, the work becomes our god. We worship at its altar. We look to it to solve all our problems. We make sacrifices to be in its presence. But as AA says, addictions are "cunning," weaving into the fabric of our lives until the source of addiction is in control.

Reflection: Have you tangled with any addictions on your spiritual journey? Have you been released from them? Tell the story.

Release from addiction is essentially a conversion experience. Some conversion experiences, such as Bill W.'s, are sudden and dramatic, changing one's life in a forceful and emotional moment. This type of experience fits our stereotype of "conversion." But for most addicts, the conversion experience is more subtle and quiet. It is a conversion nonetheless.

Great spiritual stories often include moments of conversion. Merton's *The Seven Storey Mountain* and C. S. Lewis's *Mere Christianity* come to mind as two powerful widely known spiritual autobiographies that include strong elements of conversion.

William James gave us a concise and helpful definition of conversion as "the process, gradual or sudden, by which a self hitherto divided, and consciously wrong inferior and unhappy, becomes unified and consciously right superior and happy, in consequence of its firmer hold upon religious realities" (*The Varieties of Religious Experience. P*enguin: New York, 1958, p. 157). It strikes me, by the way, that a conversion experience is often what persons, both clients and therapists, seek from psychotherapy.

My own conversion experience was of the gradual type, although when I got up that morning of June 2, 1983, there was a strong sense that something internal had shifted.

Reflection: Have conversion experiences been a facet of your journey? If so, describe them.

The journey to sobriety did not stop with my attending AA meetings. Persons in recovery are also called to the Twelve Steps, a plan of action that recognizes that stopping addictions is not sufficient if one's goal is health at every level. Basically the Twelve Steps are divided into four sections. The first sections, Steps 1 through 3, are intended to help the addict get his/her spiritual house in order. Steps 4 through 7 involve cleaning one's psychological house. Steps 8 and 9 involve cleaning up the interpersonal wreckage left in the path of addiction. The final three steps are maintenance steps, activities intended to be done on an ongoing basis to maintain and enhance sobriety.

The third step suggests that addicts turn their "will and their lives over to the care of the God of their understanding." I have struggled mightily with this step, in part because of my lifelong struggle with the theme of suffering. Is every detail of one's life a part of a Divine Plan, as AA seems to suggest, or is a Divine Presence concerned mainly about the Big Picture with details left to us, as George Burns suggests in the film *Oh God!?* I don't know. To get past this third step, I had to do something. Given my doubts, the best that I could do was to acknowledge that I would make a sincere effort to turn my life and my will over. I've not always been successful, at times bothered by doubts and at times just stubborn.

Catholic that I am, I also struggled with the moral inventory of the fourth step. After weeks, I found myself ruminating over it, trying to uncover every sordid detail. In essence, I was trying to develop a perfect fourth step. Finally, I shared my dilemma in a meeting and one crusty old-timer said, "Why don't you just get the damned thing over with?" This represents one of the things I love about AA. People have a way of cutting through intellectual B.S. and getting to the heart of the matter. Why not indeed? I made a call to my friend Father Stephen Peters, to complete my fifth step which is the sharing of the fourth step with another person. The power of confession. And so I opted to do my fifth step as a confession with a priest I trusted.

Reflection: Have you had any positive experiences with any form of confession?

The sixth and seventh steps invite the addict to turn character defects over to God for healing. And so I opted to turn over my bad temper. I made this decision on Ash Wednesday and felt very good about my resolve. Later that day I stood at my window watching an ice cream man peddle his wares—in front of my house! With his customers scattering their wrappers on *my lawn!!* I stood fuming until the dam broke. I exploded from my house, confronting the ice cream man with curses and threats. Puzzled, he remained calm and suggested that I allow him to finish with his customers prior to discussing the matter further. His calmness humbled me. When he came to speak to me, the condition of my lawn had become trivial. But he promised to survey it after finishing with his customers. Then he gave me a box of fudgesicles. I felt about two inches tall. "So much for God healing me. Thanks a lot!"

Later that year I visited my parents. My dad commented on how I seemed to be calmer. And so it was that God did indeed start healing me, but I had to get my ego out of the way first!

Reflection: Have you had any prayers answered in ways you didn't recognize? What role has humility played in your spiritual journey?

I had grown up with a picture of humility to mean being bowed over in a subservient role of some sort. I suppose at some level I also understood humility to mean some awareness of one's sinfulness. The scribes and Pharisees, after all, were not humble. This seventh step experience added another dimension to my understanding. Humility, I saw, was the recognition of one's ego in action, getting in the way, holding onto control. Someone in AA once defined ego to mean "edging God out." I indeed called upon God for help, then muscled my way into the deal, trying to orchestrate the healing. God apparently needed to get me out of the way and the only way to do this was to use an angel in the form of an ice cream man to flatten my ego.

Humility is a key facet of recovery and is a critical trait for the spiritual journey. Without a humble attitude, we can easily slip into an "us-them" mentality in which the "us" is clearly superior. I have come to understand that truly humble people can point to ways in which they are gifted. Humility is nothing more and nothing less than a balanced view of oneself as both saint and sinner.

Reflection: What are your gifts? What are your major character defects? If you struggle with either question, you may be far from humility.

The eighth and ninth steps have to do with making amends. Not just saying "Whoops! Sorry!" but being prepared to make things right if requested. Making amends, I realized, also included the willingness to listen to the other person's pain without defending oneself. Not an easy task. I was fortunate that each person on my list accepted my amends with welcome and support. Perhaps the most touching response came from my then seven-year-old son Ben who, after I asked for his forgiveness, simply nodded his head and said, "I love you, Dad." (Ben, by the way, also cut to the bottom line very quickly when I first mentioned to him that I was not drinking beer. He simply said, "Good," then went about his business.)

The final three steps are maintenance steps involving maintaining my relationship with God and those around me as well as reaching out to others caught up in addiction.

I was reading about actor Kirk Douglas the other day. He rightly takes pride in the role he played in breaking the Hollywood blacklist. Perhaps he considers hiring Dalton Trumbo to do the script for *Spartacus* as a defining moment in his life. A defining moment is an event that both reflects and shapes who each of us is. For me, it was the first time I walked into an AA meeting.

All twelve steps have been a great adventure and comprise one of the most significant stretches of my own spiritual journey. During times of doubt, I touch upon that morning of June 2, 1983. It's the clearest evidence I have of God touching my life.

Reflection: What are some defining moments in your life?

CHAPTER 15

On Silence

Two significant events happened in the fall of 1986. First of all, the Boston Red Sox lost the World Series in a most tragic fashion. Second, I had the privilege and joy of attending a weeklong retreat directed by two of my spiritual mentors—Morton Kelsey and John Sanford.

The retreat was sponsored by the Benedictine community of Pecos, New Mexico, and was conducted at a nearby Baptist retreat center. A true ecumenical event! In any case, I looked forward to time alone, figuring that I would get into some heavy-duty journal work and reflection.

After my traveling companions and I arrived at the center, we parted company and I headed for my room. What greeted me there was—silence. Terrifying, all-encompassing silence. My first reaction to the silence was a familiar one. I wanted to drink.

I knew early in life that silence was powerful. My mother, when she was angry, would not speak. Those of us on the receiving end of this tactic would feel quite powerless. During my later training in Rogerian psychotherapy, I realized that the silences which are often a part of client-centered therapy were very powerful, creating significant pressure on the client to work, to speak, to do something! But the silence with which I was confronted in Pecos was more than uncomfortable.

Why can silence be so terrifying? Doris Grumback expresses the terror in a most vivid manner: "One must go into himself armed to the teeth but also wearing a full plate of armor. . . . Even so protected, one is still not safe from assault by the guerrilla forces of painful memories and deeply hidden guilt" (*Fifty Days of Solitude.* Beacon Press: Boston, 1994, p. 91). Or as she says more succinctly "Absolute silence becomes noisy" (*ibid,* p. 61).

A capacity for solitude and silence is necessary on the spiritual highway. Without them, it is all too easy to avoid that within each of us that needs to be faced. Henri Nouwen suggested, ". . . silence is the discipline by which the inner fire of God is tended and kept alive" (*The Way of the Heart.* Ballantine: New York, 1983, p. 37).

Perhaps you have experienced a night in the woods. John Muir wrote, "When one is alone at night in the death of these woods, the stillness is at once awful and sublime. Every leaf seems to speak" (*The Wilderness World of John Muir.* Houghton Mifflin: Boston, 1954, p. 313). When in the presence of silence, then, we are challenged first of all to listen. In the woods at night, a child can be a great teacher, for he or she will hear every creak or crunch or growl, demanding to know, "What was that, Dad?" When we venture inward, we too hear creaks and growls.

Reflection: Have you ever been frightened or intimidated by silence?

In earlier times such as the retreats I'd taken, silence was a welcome respite, a peaceful haven wherein I could pray and feel very close to God. It was in silence that I first had glimmers of the mystical domain.

Reflection: When has silence been positive and spiritually meaningful for you?

In Pecos, I was met with the dark side of silence. What do we meet on such dark alleys? As noted above, we encounter that about which we are ashamed. We encounter the vestiges of unhealed wounds, lurking amidst painful memories. If we attempt to sit in silence, doing nothing other than listening, we may encounter our compulsions. The need to be productive. The need to be working on *something!* As I did, we may also confront our addictions.

And so we may go to great lengths to avoid silence. To fill our days with noise. Anthony O'Hear, writing in the *Wall Street Journal,* observed the ease with which we can avoid silence, thanks to modern technology: "The Walkman was the first assault on the Bastille of quiet reflection, blasting music—rarely great music—into a mind that would otherwise be alone with its thoughts. With the cell phone, the old regime fell. The cell phone . . . can clearly destroy what is left of unmolested thought by making unnecessary, babble-filled conversation always and everywhere possible" ("The Soundness of Silence," *The Wall Street Journal.* May 5, 2000, p. W17).

Reflection: In what ways do you avoid silence?

There are many faces of silence. Terrifying. Comforting. Inviting. And then there is a special type of silence.

About a year ago, I sat with a friend who was dying of AIDS. He shared some tears, grieving all of life that he loved and of which he was about to let go. Friends. Books he'd not get to. Music yet to be heard. And then we sat in silence as he allowed me to hold his hand. Even more than his sharing, that silence was a moment of deep intimacy.

Reflection: In what ways has silence enriched your experiences of intimacy?

CHAPTER 16

Our Image of God

Perhaps you can remember where you first heard about God. I cannot. I have a vague memory of attending Mass at some early point in my life. I vaguely recall being bored and restless. One of my earliest memories centers around the Bible we had in our house. It had reproductions of classical paintings including one of Abraham about to slaughter his son. I found those pictures both horrifying and fascinating. I didn't understand anything about the tricky theological issues inherent in that event. (Personally, I often wonder what the conversation coming down from the mountain was like. "What was that all about, Pa?"—something along those lines.) So I'm fairly certain that my early image of God was indeed the stereotypic bearded Anglo-Saxon character with a rather fierce look in His eyes.

Reflection: What are some of your early spiritual memories? What was your image of God when you were little?

My own image of God had been fairly static and negative until I underwent therapy. Then I began to experience a healing side of God. Through John Sanford's *The Kingdom Within* I saw that God could be a profound and insightful psychologist. And the God that I met the first day of my sobriety was clearly a God of grace and miracles.

But the God of my understanding that evolved during the 1980s still had residual qualities of the God of my childhood. I still feared going to hell. I still had some mixed-up notions about what sin is. And the God of that time was clearly a man.

Thomas Merton once wrote, "Our image of God tells us more about ourselves than about Him" (*New Seeds of Contemplation.* New Directions: New York, 1961, p. 1). The God that I have believed in reflected my fears and my great struggles with letting go. Even in recovery, I might have stayed stuck with that image; however, in 1987 I attended a workshop given by Matthew Linn, Dennis Linn, and Sheila Fabricant. These gentle kind souls introduced an idea that to me was revolutionary—the idea of God as female. This possibility was introduced within the context of exploring the notion that the image of God that we have acquired is mediated by human beings, especially our fathers, and therefore may be in need of some healing. The doorway the Linns and Ms. Fabricant proposed was to image God as a loving mother.

The image of God as loving mother had simply never occurred to me! The imagery I experienced was of a loving, nurturing God, the kind of God whom in many ways I'd grown to long for. This healing essentially allowed me to break free from the confining image of God as a man. This in turn allowed me to image God in many ways, not just as a woman.

Reflection: What is your image of God at this point in your life? Who are some of the people who influenced this image?

I had learned through AA that I would benefit spiritually if I developed my own understanding of God. But it was not until this workshop that I realized how confining the image was that I'd grown up with.

The second major shift in my image of God came more slowly. Influenced by Teilhard de Chardin and by Jungian analyst Fritz Kunkel, I began to sense a God whose acts of creation did not stop after seven days. I came to believe in a God who continues to create and looks to each of us to participate in this creation.

Teilhard was both priest and scientist. He did not automatically reject the concept of evolution. In fact, he developed an astounding theory that viewed evolution from a spiritual perspective and viewed God as actively involved in the process of evolution. In essence, he viewed creation as ongoing. He wrote: "We may perhaps imagine that creation was finished long ago. But that would be quite wrong. It continues still more magnificently, and at the highest levels of the world. . . . And we serve to complete it, even by the humblest work of our hands" (*The Divine Milieu.* Harper & Row: New York, 1960, p. 62). Teilhard goes on to say: ". . . in action I adhere to the creative power of God; I coincide with it; I become not only its instrument but its living extension" (*Ibid,* p. 62). What a revolutionary notion! No wonder Teilhard got into trouble.

This notion has further been explored from a variety of perspectives. Fritz Kunkel wrote about creation continuing from an intrapsychic perspective (*Creation Continues.* Word Books: Waco, TX 1973). The immanence of

God's creation runs through Ian Bradley's suggestion of God as Green and therefore active in *all* of creation (*God is Green: Ecology for Christians.* Image: New York, 1990). Charles Cummings, another ecological theologian, gives us an interesting twist on evolution: "Evolution becomes another term for the ongoing creative activity of God by which all beings are supported in the cosmic dance and gently directed to their goal" (*Eco-Spirituality: Toward a Reverent Life.* Paulist: Mahwah, NJ, 1991, p. 10). And God's active creative presence is found in the rediscovery of the centuries-old Celtic Christianity. (See, for example, Anthony Duncan, *The Elements of Celtic Christianity.* Element Books: Shaftesbury, Doset, Great Britain, 1992.)

Participating in God's creation can be an intimidating idea. It at least makes sense that we should not get in the way. Thus, the notion of God's creation continuing has had direct impact on my beliefs about just how important it is to pursue a lifestyle of peace. To do otherwise would seem to interfere with the manner in which my neighbor participates in God's creation.

I've come to believe something else about us as humans. Some years ago my friend Dick Park invited me to participate in a workshop on journaling. As an experiment, I decided I would present a "mini-course" on writing poetry and then invite participants to share their poems. At that time the result was surprising. Many participants produced and shared poems. Many of the poems shared were quite profound. Beyond that, many of the participants were pleasantly surprised to discover this inner poet. I have done this exercise often since then and always with the same result—profound poems and pleasantly surprised participants. This pattern has convinced me that one of the ways in which we participate in God's creation is by embracing and expressing our artistic creativity.

As Julia Cameron writes in *The Artist's Way* (J. P. Tarcher, 1992), one of the greatest impediments to our creativity is the judgment we pass on the products of our creative efforts. This tends to be fear-based because the products of our creativity are very personal and so, when we contemplate sharing them, we become afraid. I know in my case with each of the books I've written, I always was excited to receive the first box of books. But upon opening the box, each time I felt a little panic. I realized that the publication of the book made me feel vulnerable to criticism, to judgment.

There are so many ways we can participate in God's creation. Writing poems is certainly one way. But there are so many others. The arts as we typically think of them. Cooking. Gardening. Designing a room. Playing with a child. The possibilities are vast, for the creative God is a God of abundance.

Reflection: How do you express your creativity? If you have no creative expressions, what gets in the way?

CHAPTER 17

On Midlife

Midway in our life's journey,
I went astray from the straight road
and woke to find myself alone in a dark wood.
How shall I say what wood that was!
I never saw so drear,
so rank, so arduous a wilderness!
Its very memory gives a shape to fear.

Death could scarce be more bitter than that place!
But since it came to good, I will recount
all that I found revealed there by God's grace.

—Dante Alighieri

Thus begins Dante's descent into hell as retold in his epic *The Inferno* (translated by John Ciardi, Mentor. New York, 1954, p. 28), a poem written by Dante as he traversed the midpoint of his own life. Dante's words point to the tumultuous, even frightening passage through midlife. The legacy of his poetry gives testimony to the gifts which midlife can reveal. Truly an experience of hellish and heavenly proportions!

I turned forty in 1988 and had already gone through one midlife crisis in 1983.

Midlife crisis has a bad reputation, thanks in large part to made-for-television movies that typically portray a man in his forties involved with a woman much younger than him and/or making a drastic change in employment. Such portrayals are rarely sympathetic and often end with the man "coming to his senses," returning to home and job. But I will be arguing here that midlife crisis is a process of tremendous significance and potential, that it impacts men *and* women, that it calls into play serious issues in need of attention and perhaps healing, and that it is a process that is spiritual in nature. Midlife crisis and the manner in which we confront it shape the quality and even content of the second half of life.

Listen to some of the symptoms of midlife crisis as articulated by Brewi and Brennan (1991): “Lethargy, apathy, monotony, indifference, impotence, frigidity, uncertainty, listlessness, dawdling over tasks, loss of interest in things that were once of vital concern; going through the motions, boredom . . . ” (*Mid-life: Psychological and Spiritual Perspectives.* Crossroad: New York, 1991, p. 35). And also “regret, anger, self-doubt, doubt about all relationships and commitments, religious doubt, anxiety, threat; feeling imprisoned, trapped, desperate, hopeless, tortured, hemmed in, restless, dissatisfied, morose, melancholy, nauseous, despairing, fearful . . .” (*ibid.,* p. 39).

The turmoil of midlife is perhaps expressed best by a paradoxical word—*stagnant.* We may feel stagnant at midlife. Standing still, no energy or movement, no life stirring within. Stagnant water quite simply has a stink to it, doesn’t it?

As I mentioned, midlife process and crisis is a spiritual event. Not necessarily, however, a religious event. In fact, the turmoil of midlife can wreak havoc on whatever religious beliefs one might be clinging to.

What is it that is going on at midlife? Psychiatrist Carl Jung was an early observer of this significant event and used it as a pivotal point in expanding upon Freud’s emphasis of childhood. Jung wrote: “The afternoon of human life must also have a significance of its own and cannot be merely a pitiful appendage to life’s morning. The significance of morning undoubtedly lies in the development of the individual, our entrenchment in the outer world, the propagation of our kind, and the care of our children. . . .Whoever carried over into the afternoon of life the law of the morning. . . . must pay for doing so with damage to his soul (*Modern Man in Search of a Soul.* Harcourt, Brace, and World: New York, 1933, p. 109).

In other words, at midlife the rules of the game change. Whereas the first half of life focuses on growth and achievement, the second half calls for a turning inward, in part because we must set many inner matters on hold during life’s first half so that we might move forward. As Edward Whitmont notes, “The bill will now be presented for what was by-passed in the earlier years. Whatever was left behind because it was not suitable for external adaptation, for success and practical use, demands now to be heard and realized” (*The Symbolic Quest: Basic Concepts of Analytic Psychology.* Princeton University Press: Princeton, N.J., 1969, p. 283).

Reflection: What have your experiences of midlife been so far?

Certain events and processes can precipitate midlife crisis or at least move along the process of midlife. Let us turn to a consideration of these events:

1. A specific age. While midlife need not be defined by a number, nonetheless your own arrival at midlife may be heralded by a number of significance to you. For many people, this number is forty. For others, it may be thirty-five or fifty. Or, if you are Jack Benny, thirty-nine. The impact of a number may certainly reflect a self-fulfilling prophecy, i.e., the thought that I'll probably have a midlife crisis when I turn forty can end up precipitating one. For others, however, there may simply be a stunning moment of realization and disbelief when we reflect, "My God, I'm forty years old! When did that happen?"

Reflection: What ages—past, present, or future—do you regard as significant on your journey?

2. Loss of a loved one. The closer death strikes to us, the more our own mortality is dramatized. Further, when one's parent or parents die, there is a sense of the closing out of a generation—the one right ahead of us. This means that one's own generation is the next likely focus for dying.

Reflection: How have the losses of loved ones impacted upon you?

3. Another death which bears significance. Sometimes it is not the passing of a loved one that precipitates midlife process; it may be the death of someone whom we do not know personally but whose passing in some way represents deep loss. For me and for many men at midlife, the death of Mickey Mantle is an example. Mickey Mantle brought us back to our youth. We might remember desperate efforts to obtain his baseball card or listening to his exploits via the voice of Mel Allen or, if we were lucky (as I was on two occasions), actually seeing the Mick play at Yankee Stadium. With his passing, it seemed, our youth had finally left as well.

Reflection: What deaths of persons not known to you personally have nonetheless had impact on you?

4. Physical changes/health problems. The midlife process is triggered for some women by menopause and for some men by prostate problems. These events do not, however automatically trigger midlife crisis. Other physical changes that mark aging can also creep up on us. Gray hair. Wrinkles. Stiff joints in the morning. Something that we notice that brings to mind forcefully the thought, "I'm getting old!" Health problems often associated with age may trigger midlife emotions. Hypertension is a case in point. Other health problems may simply dramatize one's vulnerability.

Reflection: Have you dealt with health problems or physical changes of note? How have such events affected you?

5. Growth and departure of children. The proverbial "empty nest" is a significant transition. It redefines roles and can force attention to neglected issues and relationships which were set aside during child-rearing years. I recall returning home with my wife after we had taken our twin sons to faraway Minnesota for college. They were our youngest children and so the nest was now empty. When we returned home, we sat down for our first meal alone. I remember looking across the table at my wife and thinking, "This would be an awful moment if I didn't like this person." It is at such moments that some persons recognize that they have drifted far apart, possibly to the point where they feel like strangers.

Reflection: If you have children, how has their departure affected you?

We can conceptualize midlife as involving crises along any or all of three domains: intimacy, vitality, and legacy. Within the three areas there are common themes, most of which we've already encountered at this stage of the journey. These themes are: woundedness, grieving, sex, and the "Shadow."

Woundedness

We have already touched on the notion of woundedness, noting that most of us are wounded in one way or another, some more deeply than others. Many of us try to avoid our wounds, hoping that over time the related pain will "go away." At midlife, some of these wounds may begin throbbing from inattention, demanding to be dealt with. The story of the Fisher King illustrates this aspect of midlife. (See Robert Johnson, *The Fisher King and the Handless Maiden* [Harper: San Francisco, 1993] for an introduction to this mythic story.)

The legend of the Fisher King is found in the story of Percival and his quest for the Holy Grail. It was also the subject of the recent film of the same name starring Jeff Bridges and Robin Williams (1991). The film places an interesting twist to the story and so we will incorporate this twist into the current telling:

A young king goes off into the forest, seeking that which will make him a man. He comes upon a fire and, within the fire, he beholds the Holy Grail. He reaches for the cup, which vanishes, and he becomes badly burned. As time passes, his wound deepens. He spends his days fishing and his nights groaning. A fool wanders into the castle of the Fisher King and finds the king thirsty. He hands the Kkng a cup of water. And the cup he hands the king is the Holy Grail, that for which the king has been longing.

At midlife, much like the Fisher King, we can become overwhelmed by that which hurts within us. We look for relief, even healing, but overlook the reality that quite often that for which we seek is already at hand. We just don't recognize it.

Reflection: What wounds have you avoided?

Grieving

Midlife involves a time of loss and coming to terms with losses. Some of the types of losses have already been mentioned—children leaving home, a loss of health, etc. However, some of the grieving of midlife may also include grief which has been deferred from the time of loss. Thus, we may find ourselves grieving over relationships broken some years ago. We may need to grieve a loss of idealism. As with grief at any stage of life, the task is to face the grief and accept the loss. Avoidance only prolongs the pain and keeps us from moving on.

Reflection: What losses are you grieving at this time? What losses might you be avoiding?

Sex

Sex is a powerful midlife theme, in part because we may be prone to gravitate to sex as a solution for much of our midlife distress. Sex can give us the appearance of intimacy. It can, for a few moments, open or reopen the door to passion. And in some ways we may turn to sex to give us the illusion of being young forever.

Reflection: If you are experiencing or have experienced midlife, write about where you are/were sexually at that point in your life. Satisfied? Frustrated? Mechanical?

The Shadow

As we have seen earlier, the Shadow is not necessarily negative. It represents the Inner Self's quest for completion and balance. Stephen A. Diamond expresses the potential of the Shadow more forcefully: "That which we have previously run from and rejected turns out to be the redemptive source of vitality, creativity and authentic spirituality" ("Redeeming our devils and demons" in C. Zweig & J. Abrams' *Meeting the Shadow: The Hidden Power of the Dark Side of Human Nature.* Jeremy P. Tarcher: New York, 1991, p.186).

I recall counseling with a very good, peace-loving man involved in action for social justice. He also happened to be at midlife. He was troubled by a dream he kept having in which he was at a party. Suddenly, an intruder entered the party and began to fight with him. He always beat the daylights out of the intruder, a fact which he found most troubling to the point that he began to question the honesty of his involvement in the peace movement. We discussed the Shadow and I assured him that his acceptance of "the intruder," if anything would make him even more appreciative of peace. Interestingly, as he worked with this theme, the dreams began to change. Initially, he still beat up the intruder but then he would try to help him up. Finally, the intruder would enter the room and they would simply look at one another without violence. They weren't necessarily friends but they were at peace.

Many of our meetings with the Shadow are like this. The Shadow humbles us. When we meet and make peace with our Shadow, we may grow from the encounter but are not always thrilled by what we learn.

These themes of midlife wind their way through the three faces of crisis: intimacy, vitality, and legacy.

Through the crisis of intimacy, we question the quality of our relationships. We may suddenly become aware of an absence of intimacy in our marriage. We may become aware of how we have sacrificed friendship in the name of achievement. We may simply feel very lonely. The stereotypic midlife affair can be a poor attempt to solve this crisis.

Through the crisis of vitality, we confront two issues. One is the reality that we are beginning to wind down physically. Illness, less energy, or simply aches and pains are testimony to the harsh reality that our bodies are slowly but surely dying. We also may confront an absence of or loss of passion in our lives. This aspect of the vitality crisis is not confined to sexual passion. We may become aware of a loss of ideals. Or, more simply, our lives may lack enthusiasm about much of anything.

Finally, the crisis of legacy forces us to face up to a lack of or loss of meaning in our lives. What may have seemed so important to us in the first half of life suddenly feels insignificant. We also become concerned about what will live after us. How will my time here on earth be marked?

Reflection: Write about the impact of the themes of intimacy, vitality, and legacy at the midpoint of your life.

Resolution of Midlife Turmoil

A key to resolving midlife turmoil is to accept responsibility for it. We are quick to blame, a tendency that seems to be increasing in a society that more and more fosters victim roles. The stance of victim only prolongs midlife's storms. We need to face whatever messes we've generated, assume responsibility for the wreckage and for what we've avoided, then undertake the task of healing and growing. No one can do this kind of work for someone else.

Reflection: Who do you blame for your woes? (Come on. We all blame somebody just a little. What matters now is to be aware.)

Midlife involves facing loss. Resolution involves accepting those losses.

A third important theme of midlife resolution is to simplify. One of the things we typically recognize at midlife is that our lives have become complicated. This is due to the drive to achieve. It is also due to a gradual encroaching emphasis on "stuff." We become concerned with having all sorts of "stuff." I recall an ad recently for plastic containers. It portrays a family who has too much stuff. So they buy these containers and then gleefully realize that they now have room for more stuff! At midlife, we may become appalled not only by the amount of stuff we have but about the extent of our attachment to that stuff.

The resolution of midlife involves the discovery and acknowledgement of true power and wisdom. It is my belief that our real power lies in our gifts, but that because of either false humility or real self-hatred, we are often unable to identify these gifts. Sometimes we don't like the responsibility that accompanies a gift. I recall a dream I had during the midst of my second midlife crisis at age forty. I was hiking and carrying a beautiful walking stick. The stick was as tall as me (six-foot-three) and was polished, a true work of art. I came to a bridge and, in a scene right out of Robin Hood, saw a dark figure on the bridge also with a long stick. I realized that to cross the bridge I would have to battle this person. This didn't really bother me, but as I prepared to step out onto the bridge I set down my stick, not wanting it to be "banged up." I struggled with this dream and especially with the meaning of the symbol of the stick. Finally, while sculpting the image with clay, it came to me. Power! The stick represented my own power, my gifts. And the dream was confronting me, telling me that I jealously guarded my gift, not putting it into battle. What was the gift? I believe it was the ability to write. And so the dream challenged me not only to write but also to share what I wrote, knowing that I may face criticism.

Indeed, the midlife crisis may be considered resolved when one has uncovered the gift brought by the crisis. The gift is one from the soul as Murray Stein notes: "When the soul awakens at midlife and presents its gifts, life is permanently marked by inclusion of them. Taken in, they become the hallmark of your life, the core of your uniqueness. Refused, they can haunt your days and may undermine all your toiling" (*In Midlife: A Jungian Perspective.* Spring Publications: Woodstock, CT, 1983, p. 5). Note the warning. A gift refused doesn't go away. Its dark side can become most bothersome.

Midlife crisis has a fundamental spiritual quality to it. We are struggling with potent spiritual issues. All the themes you have explored so far on this journey of spiritual autobiography fall into scrutiny at midlife. Understanding this also plays a key role in resolving midlife.

Finally, midlife may draw to completion when all of us, men and women, embrace a particular image.

At the conclusion of the film *Braveheart,* narrator Mel Gibson describes the victory of Scottish peasants at Bannokbane. He says, "They fought like warrior-poets." I found that image very striking. A warrior poet. At first, it seemed almost a contradiction. But then I recalled Jung's statement that the ultimate task of development was for men to integrate their female side and for women to incorporate their male side into the full personality. This, then, is the image of the warrior-poet. A person capable of waging battle when necessary yet also able to simply pause and appreciate. We are all called to become warrior poets.

One final caution. There are no solutions here, no fake magic to give the illusion of coming out of the forest. But take heart from the words of Abraham Twerski who reveals one of the many paradoxes of aging: "To be forever striving for knowledge, for new insights, for fresh perspectives, that is the way we can take youth along far into our biologic old age" (*Generation to Generation: Personal Recollections of a Chassidic Legacy.* Traditional Press: Brooklyn, 1985, p. 42).

Reflection: In what ways are you a Warrior-Poet?

CHAPTER 18

On Teachers

I have mentioned several times that each of our journeys is a community project. My own journey belongs not just to me. It belongs to my sisters. To the Jesuits. To the friends of Bill W. But it belongs especially to a group of persons whom I view as some of my finest teachers. These are people who each allowed me to accompany them on a significant portion of their journeys. They allowed me to accompany them as they prepared to die. (Where each story begins with a name in quotations, the person's name has been changed as have certain identifying details.)

"Mary"

Mary was my first teacher of the final mile. My wife knew her through theater, and she was a vibrant lady, a real-life "Mame." She called me from the hospital and asked me to visit, informing me that she'd been diagnosed with cancer and had been given six months to live. If you remember the musical "Mame," you can imagine Mary's reaction to the prognosis. She was determined to set the prognosis on its ear. She sought help initially with managing pain.

Some time after she left the hospital, her son accompanied her to a session. He mentioned with simultaneous anger and amusement that he had a problem with how his mother had informed him of her illness. Mary interrupted and said, "For you to understand, I have to tell you a joke. There were two brothers and one was going to Europe so he asked brother number two to watch his cat. While in Europe brother one called and asked, "How's the cat?" Brother two said, "She's dead." Well, brother one was upset by his brother's bluntness. "You could have broken it to me gradually" he explained. "The first day I called, when I asked about the cat, you could have said, 'Well, she's out on the roof and won't come in.' Then the next time you could have said, 'She's still out on the roof.' Then maybe the third time you could have told me she died." A year later brother number one again went to

Europe and called his brother. "How's Mom?" brother one said. Brother two paused, then replied, "Uh, . . . she's out on the roof!"

Darn good joke. Mary's son interjected, saying, "So Mom calls me up and says "Well, son, I'm out on the roof!"

I had Mary read *Getting Well Again* by O. Carl Simonton (Bantam: New York, 1992). This is a recovery program for cancer patients that, among other things, uses imagery to combat the illness. Mary liked the approach and found it helpful. This, I assumed, was where I fit in to her battle.

Over the next two years, Mary would check in with me from time to time. "When I'm in trouble," she said, "I check in with you and God. Not necessarily in that order." She worried over how her children were dealing with her illness. She grieved over shortened time with her grandchildren. Mary had smashed the prognosis and had been able to return to her job as an advertising executive.

Her son called me one day to let me know that Mary was back in the hospital and that the doctors could no longer do anything for her. That evening I went to see her. When I entered the room, she said simply, "What do I do now?" I asked her what she'd like to do and she said "Face it." We talked of her legacy of courage to her grandchildren. We talked of the fine battle she waged. Finally, she looked at me and said, "Would you like to know how you helped me?" This is a rare offer to a therapist, so I took her up on it. She smiled, took my hand, and said, "You helped me face this without bitterness." I'd thought all this time it had been the imagery work. What a great gift she gave me! Three days later she died as the sun was rising.

Reflection: In what ways are you passionate about life?

____

____

____

____

____

____

"Alma"

Alma was a lovely thirty-year-old woman who was a counselor herself. She came to my office and stated that she'd been diagnosed with cancer and given less than a year to live. She requested help dealing with the emotions she knew she'd face on this journey. That first visit she mentioned that her greatest regret was that she wouldn't live long enough to hear her infant son tell her he loved her.

Alma proved to be an honest, deeply spiritual woman. She'd been raised Catholic but had been away from the church for some years. One day she expressed the regret that, because she'd been away from the church, she would not be eligible for a Catholic funeral Mass. I asked her if she might want to receive the sacrament of reconciliation. Like most Catholics, she'd had some bad experiences in the confessional and so she hesitated. I referred her to a priest who I was reasonably sure would receive her without judgment. At her subsequent session, she relayed a very positive healing encounter with this priest. She felt reconnected to her church.

Alma worked with imagery and also had a fighter's attitude. She, too, smashed the prognosis but endured much physical pain in the process. As with most of the other teachers mentioned here, I often felt powerless, and one day I shared with Alma that I felt powerless in the face of her cancer. The following session she made reference to this statement. She gently said, "You know, I don't expect you to do anything about the cancer. I just need a safe place where I can do cancer talk."

One day some two years after we started, Alma came in. She was now without hair and walking with a cane, the cancer beginning to attack her bones. But on this day she smiled. When I asked her what the smile was about, she said "This morning my son told me he loved me." She added that those words made the fighting and the pain all worth it. A few weeks later, she died at home.

Reflection: Consider your loved ones. Are there any words that are unspoken that need to be said to any of them?

"Anne"

I'd known Ann slightly before I went to see her at the hospital. Her mother had been a client for a short while and she and her family attended the same church I did. She had begun to complain of swelling and pain in her arm. It went misdiagnosed for some time. When I first saw her in the hospital, she sought help with pain. A short time after that first meeting, she received the diagnosis of non-Hodgkin's lymphoma. She was twenty-one years old.

Approximately one year after her diagnosis, Ann was offered the opportunity for a bone marrow transplant. She went to San Antonio full of hope. Weeks later the verdict was in. The transplant had not been a success. The cancer was back. I visited Ann the day she received the news. She raged, throwing pillows around the room as she yelled, "I don't want to die!" She fumed at God. Later she would express guilt about being angry with God, she of such beautiful young faith. I tried to assure her that God could take her anger.

One Monday in September she called and asked me if there was any book I could recommend for her to get her mother. I suggested *Seeds of Hope* by Henri Nouwen and said I'd check the local bookstore for her. There was one copy left which I dropped off at her house on my way home. I later learned that she directed her sister to go ahead and give their mother the book since "I might not be here for Mom's birthday."

The next night I received a call from Ann's mother asking if I could come to their home. She explained that she thought Ann was preparing to die. I found Ann to be restless and having some trouble breathing. Some relaxation imagery helped, and I went home shortly after midnight. Ann's mother called me again at 5:00 A.M. Ann was struggling with her breathing. As I sat by her bed, I noticed that the sun was rising. I remembered Mary's passing and said to Ann, "The sun's just coming up, Ann. This is a good time to go to Jesus." At that, she sat bolt upright, a sort of final roar, I think. Then she slowly lay back down. Over the next ten minutes, her breathing slowed, then finally stopped. The last words she had said to me the night before were, "Is Mom OK?"

Her funeral testified to the fact that, for such a young person, she'd touched a great many lives. As a gift, her mother gave me a picture of Ann—dressed as a clown, gently blowing a balloon to an unseen child.

Reflection: Consider your loved ones again. Are there any actions in connection with any of them that you have been putting off?

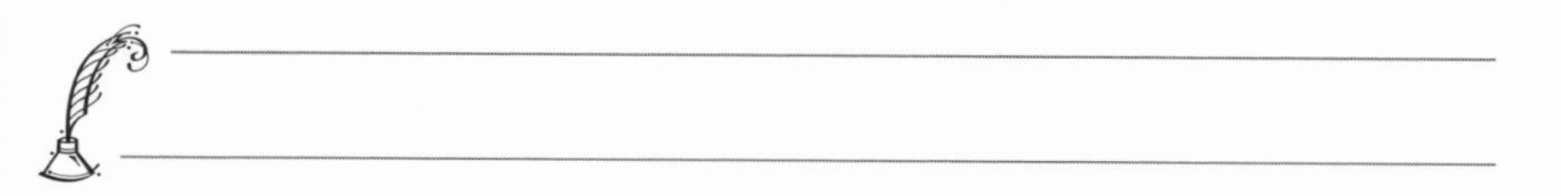

____

____

____

____

____

____

____

____

____

____

The Children of Camp Courageous

> "The world is wide and beautiful.
> But almost everywhere, everywhere, the children are dying."
>
> —*Edward Abbey*
> (*A Voice Crying in the Wilderness.*
> St. Martin's Press: New York, 1989, p. 46)

In the summer of 1991, my oldest son Matt and I began attending a place called Camp Courageous. My thanks to the Board of Directors of Candlelighters of El Paso for granting me permission to share these experiences. This a camp where, for one week, he and I served as counselors. Not psychotherapy counselors but softball-playing, bracelet-making counselors. The children who attend are like any group of kids—energetic, testing limits, frustrating. However, there is one word that bound these children together—cancer. These children were waging a battle against cancer or, in a few cases, had won the battle or at least been given a reprieve.

Each year, I was assigned as a counselor to the teenage group. This allowed me the luxury of getting up earlier and running, for teenagers, thankfully, tend to greet morning with great reluctance, wanting instead to sink deeper into their sleeping bags (especially after having been up half the night). A small joy from the last two summers that I fondly remember is when some of the boys in my group actually got up a time or two to run with me. (In this regard, I'll share one of the nicest compliments I've ever received. While running with one of the boys, he turned to me and said with utter innocence, "Say, you're in pretty good shape for an old guy.")

The children we met over the course of four summers were both remarkable and typical. These teenagers, for instance, were as adept at power struggles as any I've met. The little children (with whom my son usually worked) could be as annoying and demanding as the best of them. By the same token, they could have a profound insight or perspective. At times, simply hearing them talk about their battles rendered us speechless. My son recalls coming upon four of his charges, all under seven years old, and listening to them compare stories about their experiences with portable catheters.

There is something within most of us that screams a resounding *no* to the idea of children contracting cancer. We may be horrified by the inhumanity that we inflict upon one another, yet when we hear stories of atrocities, we just sigh. But when we hear of a child diagnosed with cancer, we feel the rumble of a protest within. Such things are not supposed to happen to children, we think. At whom are we raging? Aren't we arguing with God? Absolutely! Many of my early-morning runs at Camp Courageous were taken up with angry words directed at God. Especially when I would learn that another child known from previous years had died. Such harsh realities stood in sharp contrast to the magnificent forest and Technicolor sunrises that surrounded my run.

And so it goes. I am reminded of the Tao, of the tension of opposites. Bald heads and missing limbs against a backdrop of pine trees and flowers. This seems to be the world we've been handed. Even within nature, we encounter these poles. As I wax poetic about the forest, Annie Dillard's horrifying story about the death of a frog comes back to me. Here is her description of how a water beetle kills a frog:

> "(The water beetle's) grasping forelegs are mighty and hooked inward. It seizes a victim with these legs, hugs it tight, and paralyzes it with enzymes injected during a vicious bite. That one bite is the only bite it ever takes. Through the puncture shoots the poison that dissolves the victim's muscles and bones and organs—all but the

> skin—and through it the giant water beetle sucks out its victim's body, reduced to a juice" (*Pilgrim at Tinker Creek.* Perennial Library: New York, 1985, p. 6).

This passage rivals the greatest horror writing I can think of.

In contemplating the giant water beetle, I am inclined to view it as the villain and to define what it does to the poor frog as evil. But I impose a moral judgment here. The water beetle is just being a water beetle. Cancer, too, is simply cancer. It is neither a test nor a punishment, even when the sufferer is a child.

Nature, after all, is amoral. Thus, those who sadistically argue that a disease is invoked as a punishment, whether the disease is AIDS or cancer or something else, are only imposing an ugly morality on amoral nature.

The amorality of nature, of course, does not ease our outrage. Aren't the rules of nature set up by God? Many of these children, especially the younger ones, don't waste time on such theological reflections, focusing instead on having a good time. Some of the older ones, however, will occasionally give a glimpse of their inner battles. One summer I sat with a young woman who spoke with anguish of how she could no longer dance and of how friends seemed to drift away. She spoke, too, in such a way that I knew she was preparing herself to die. And yet, poet that she was, she spoke of how, when she died, she would live on by becoming a part of the trees and the wind, and so would continue to be a part of the other children whom she'd grown to love so much.

Such wisdom from a sixteen-year-old! Sadly, this young woman died a few weeks after this conversation.

These experiences tended to deepen my outrage with God. Yet these children taught me that time is indeed of the essence. I have often taken time for granted, assuming that I have plenty left. I put off saying something or trying to heal a relationship. I allow the passage of time to cause friendships to wither. If not for these children, I still might not notice how foolish I am when I presume upon time. Certainly, adult cancer victims have also helped me to appreciate time. But the young ones have challenged my assumptions that I will live for many more years.

Suppose we all were given the same number of years to live, let's say seventy. In other words, we knew that we'd die on our seventieth birthday. How might that affect how we I live? Well, in my own case, I probably would spend roughly sixty years in self-indulgent activity and then worry about my immortal soul for the last ten years. I would quickly become very religious. These young children remind me of the absurdity of this scenario. They are the teachers of the ninetieth psalm: "Teach us to number our days aright, that we may gain wisdom of heart."

One day at camp, I walked out onto the lodge porch to find John (this child's name has been changed) standing next to a hummingbird feeder, his arm stretched out with his index finger poised by the feeder mouth. When I asked him what he was doing, without moving or looking at me, he said, "If you hold your finger out and wait long enough, a hummingbird might land on it." A chill went up my spine. A few moments later, John lowered his arm and rubbed it, looking at me and commenting, "Chemo." While he rested, I attempted to take a picture of a hummingbird at the feeder. But each time I lifted the camera to my eye, the hummingbird would dart away. John silently observed, then said, "Hold the camera to your eye and wait." I looked at him and thought to myself, "Am I in the presence of a Zen Master?" I followed his guidance and indeed captured a hummingbird on film. The next year, I returned to camp eager to show John the picture. At the meeting place, I learned that sixteen-year-old John had died two months earlier.

The Algonquian tribes had a tradition. On the evening of a loved one's death, the family would go outside, look up into the sky, and select a star to stand as the campfire of their loved one, brightly lit so that he or she could be found when the others would follow.

Each summer after John died, I had the same experience during one of my morning runs, most often on the last one for the year. As I ran, I would notice a last bright star still visible as sunrise took over the sky. Some might say that what I saw was the morning planet. But I know the truth. There is no doubt. It was John's campfire.

Reflection: How have you taken and how do you continue to take time for granted?

____

____

____

____

____

____

____

____

____

Bob D.

I met Bob in the early 1980s when I was teaching a class on statistics. He was a young, bright, articulate soldier who did extremely well in my class. Ten years later my colleague, Gail Edwards, was counseling a gay couple. One of the men approached me and asked me if I remembered him. It was Bob. Life had not been kind to him. He had aged more than one would expect from the toll of ten years. Worse yet, he was HIV positive. Gail asked me if I would be willing to provide some individual counseling for Bob. As it turned out, Bob welcomed me as a companion on his final journey.

Bob proved to be a very literate, articulate man who openly shared his spiritual struggles. He shared his impression of organized religion, for example, by relating the following story:

> There once was a very gifted gardener whose trees, flowers, and vegetables were truly beautiful. One day, a young man snuck into the garden and began to observe the gardener at work. Finally, he got up the courage to approach the gardener for guidance in growing things. The gardener gave the young man a corner of the land and showed him everything he knew about gardens. The young man did quite well and eventually, when it was the gardener's time to go, he turned over all the gardens to the young man to manage. The young

> man did well and, in fact, fame of the gardens spread far and wide, so that many others came to study the gardens. The young man in turn passed his knowledge on to others. But those who knew the original gardener would observe one thing: while subsequent gardens were quite beautiful, none ever captured the simple beauty of that original garden.

I visited Bob at his apartment after I'd been out of town. His estranged daughter called while I was there, having been told that her father was dying. Bob was short with her and seemed annoyed. After the call, I asked him what he wanted to do for his daughter in the days he had left. He paused, then said quietly, "To patiently and gently help her heal." She came for a visit and, shortly before he died, they had that healing time together.

Reflection: What persons in your life would you like to help heal if they are open to your help?

"Jim"

In 1987, a local minister approached me about counseling with a man who'd been diagnosed with AIDS. It turned out that the man he referred was already acquainted with me. We'd met at a seminar I'd presented some years earlier.

Jim was a Renaissance man—A lover of fine wines and fine literature. He allowed me to accompany him on a remarkable, thirteen-year journey. We did not meet regularly during those thirteen years; he'd come in as he felt the need, an arrangement with which we both were comfortable. We met on a regular basis shortly after his lover died of AIDS in 1989, then again during the last two years of his life.

Jim battled many demons—the loss of his lover, the appeal of drugs, the lure of despair. But this dark side was always balanced by a true joy in living. During our time together, he shared his discovery of teas, of canaries, of the art perspectives of Sister Wendy. We'd discuss literature. He became intrigued with Jung and dream interpretation. And he waged a remarkable battle against a terrible disease.

Brilliant man that he was, Jim's greatest fear was that the disease would eventually invade his brain, causing dementia. Thankfully, this never happened. Jim sought out knowledge and understanding with a passion. I joked with him that his last gesture was likely to be reaching for a book.

The disease made slow and steady incursions. Jim lost weight. He began to walk with a cane. Trips in and out of the hospital became more frequent. Yet through all of this he sought out friends and loved ones, wanting to share his journey in hopes that others might benefit.

Finally, I received a call that he was back in the hospital and wanted to see me. I went that evening. During that visit, it was that, somewhat reluctantly, Jim was ready to go. He said that he'd been waiting for a metaphor for death and that, just prior to my arrival, one had come to him. He saw himself traveling in a podlike vehicle across a mountain and then down into a lush, peaceful valley. With a metaphor in mind, he felt it was time. A few days later, Jim died.

Jim had to get in a last word. I was asked to read them at his memorial service.

Reflection: Has your journey been touched in any way by time spent with those facing death? Tell those stories.

CHAPTER 19

On Letting Go

The third step of the Twelve Step program challenges us to "let go and let God." What I see as a theme of my own story is that I am happy to "let God," but often on my terms. Thus, I have often failed at the part that has to do with "letting go." In part, I have seen that I do not always trust God. I suppose trust would come more easily if I had access to what one friend referred to as "God's operations manual." But I don't.

Annie Dillard wrote, "Do we really need more victims to remind us that we are all victims? Is this some sort of parade for which a conquering army shines up its terrible guns and rolls them up and down the streets for people to see? Do we need blind men stumbling about and little flame-faced children to remind us of what God can—and will—do?" (*Holy the Firm.* Harper and Row: New York, 1984, p. 60). So the third step calls me to trust the God who took my sisters, struck down loved ones with AIDS and cancer, and allows atrocities of the worst sort in all corners of the world. This is the God in whom I am supposed to place my trust? The simple AA answer is "Yes." It has never been that easy for me.

I have known some people of simple faith and have even written about simple faith ("The Gift of Simple Faith." Spiritual Life, 1998, V. 4, 1, pp. 10–13). I find that, rather than scoffing at simple faith from some pinnacle of intellectual enlightenment, I envy it. People I have known of simple faith were not judgmental. Did not claim to have *the truth* but rather a piece of the truth which, for them, worked, giving them comfort or hope or a belief in the power of prayer. People who proclaim an "us versus them" type of faith are not the people of simple faith who've touched me. A man dying from Lou Gehrig's disease quietly expressed the belief that his God would look after his family. My mother on her deathbed simply stated, "I'm going to see my girls." These are shining examples of simple faith.

Faith, after all, is a decision to leap across a chasm, parting company with the sure foundation of rationality. Some people leap without pausing to think twice.

This issue of letting go strikes at the heart of my spiritual autobiography and struggles, yet I have continuing evidence that letting go really does work! On those occasions when I was able to let go and let God, the outcome was always the right one—not always the one I thought I wanted, but the right one.

A recent example illustrates the point. In October of last year I had planned to run my first marathon in Cape Cod. I'd trained for several months and found myself praying that I would make it to the marathon and complete it. Two weeks before the marathon I began to get sick with asthma. Things worsened to the point that, one week before the marathon, I landed in the hospital. Initially, I refused to be admitted, in large part because I was unwilling to give up my dream of the marathon. But as I lay in the ER I realized I was being selfish. So into ICU I went. At first I implored God to heal me so that I could still run the marathon. But slowly, as the hours passed, I realized I had to let go of the marathon and my demand to run it, and just accept whatever God had in mind for me. I did not let go easily, but I did let go, accepting that I might not be able to participate.

Reflection: Have you had any spiritual experiences involving letting go and letting God?

What is it that we let go of? Clearly, it is the need to be in control. We want to influence the outcome. Does this mean that I should pray for or about nothing? No. Prayer, as we've seen, has its place, but it always needs to be balanced by the ability to let go. This is a lesson which I have not learned easily.

Much of the need for letting go can be more serious than something like running a marathon. I go through this struggle whenever my wife or one of my children is going through a difficult time or hoping for a particular outcome with some struggle in their lives. I always pray for the best outcome, yet each time I know that I must let go and let God, even when it comes to the five people I love most.

I have found some help and guidance with this struggle from Zen. Buddhism, as you saw earlier, has much to say about the negative impact of attachments. As Thich Nhat Hahn says, "When we are attached to a certain table, it is not the table that causes us to suffer. It is our attachment" (*The Heart of the Buddha's Teachings.* Broadway Books: New York, 1998, p. 21). So I am reminded that what prevents me from letting go is also that which gives rise to my suffering. Quite a paradox.

In a related way, what I also let go of is ego. Letting go is quite humbling because, to let go, I need to acknowledge all within me that resists letting go.

There is an important clue here. Struggling with letting go may indeed be a struggle with pride. Perhaps this is why the theme of letting go recurs throughout various religious traditions. Richard Rohr notes: "The spiritualities of all great world religions teach us letting go: how to step aside" (*Simplicity: The Art of Loving.* Crossroad: New York, 1992, p. 23). Rohr views impediments to letting go as having three compulsions: the compulsion to be successful, the compulsion to be right, and the compulsion to be powerful (*Ibid.,* p. 44). These compulsions suggest the attachments detailed by Buddhists. The compulsion to be successful often impels us to pursue quantity, not quality. We are driven not so much by a desire for excellence but by a fear of failing. Therefore, we are unable to perform a task to a level of excellence, and then let go of the need for a specific outcome. We tend to define success by externals—salary, possessions, and so on, and become driven by the fear that nothing is enough.

The compulsion to be right means that we are not content to express our thought rationally and honestly, then let go of the outcome. If we must be right, then we will nag, badger, berate, and persist until the opposition gives up.

But, again, fear is at the bottom, and so we are not content even when the opposition caves in.

Finally, the compulsion to be powerful typically involves a frantic pursuit of position. The notion we've seen previously that our power is in our gifts would be a foreign one to the person compulsively pursuing power. Rather, power is dependent upon position.

Reflection: Have you struggled with any compulsion for success, being right, or power?

Letting go does not mean being passive. It is being content with excellence—defining how I can best perform a certain task, fulfill a certain role—then letting go of the necessity for a specific outcome. The reward will be in the contentment with excellence.

Reflection: In what ways do you/can you be content with the pursuit of excellence and thereby let go of the need for a specific outcome?

CHAPTER 20

On Religion and Spirituality

By the close of the 1980s, I felt fairly clear that there were significant differences between religion and spirituality, just as AA suggested. I continued to remain attached to my Catholicism, but the rituals seemed hollow. My children had begun to drift away from the church, striking out on their own to find more meaningful paths.

The church certainly was suffering as the ranks of priests dwindled steadily. Vocations to the priesthood apparently were hard to come by. But then the world learned that the Catholic Church had also become the repository for deep, dark secrets. We learned that our priests included active pedophiles and, worse yet, that the church had not handled this problem in an open, healing manner. Instead, there was stonewalling of investigations, and pedophiles were dealt with by shipping them to different parts of the country.

Victims of clergy abuse came to my office—deeply wounded souls ,many of whom had lost any faith in the face of betrayal by a priest they had trusted.

The diocese was slow to respond. And so I set in motion a sequence of events that on the one hand generated a compassionate response from clergy but on the other hand resulted in my being named "an enemy of the church." When I learned that a high-ranking church official had labeled me in this way and that diocesan personnel had been encouraged to avoid me, I have to admit that I was devastated. This seemed to confirm my childhood shame and feelings of unworthiness in God's eyes. Sadly, it was another event that threatened my relationship with the church. I talked with my wife about possibly exploring other forms of worship. But I took no real action, in part, I have to admit, because of fear.

What I came to realize is that something is very wrong in the Catholic Church, and that this something isn't so much about sex (as I'd thought for many years) but rather about power. It became more apparent to me that the sense of "separateness" by which we viewed our priests, and to some extent they viewed themselves, had fostered an attachment to the dark side of power. Jason Berry, writing in his excellent and disturbing history of the pedophile scandal, observed: "Countless cases across the country have exposed a warped elitism: priests and bishops above shunning lay people below" (*Lead Us Not into Temptation: Catholic Priests and the Sexual Abuse of Children.* Doubleday: New York, 1992, p. 286).

Carl Jung's portrayal of the Shadow suggests where the heart of the problem with power can be found. Few priests, I believe, can acknowledge the appeal which power holds out for them. They thereby are at risk of abusing that power, whether through sexual misconduct or mishandling of church funds. The problem, however, is not so much with motivations for becoming a priest but, rather, the unawareness of these motives. Adolf Guggenbuhl-Craig, writing about psychotherapists, observed: "No one can act out of exclusively pure motives. Even the noblest deeds are based on pure and impure, light and dark motivations" (*Power in the Helping Professions.* Dallas, TX: Spring, 1971, pp. 10–11). The same would seem to apply to one's motives for becoming a priest. (This realization, by the way, generated some reflection on my part about my own motives for wanting to become a priest!)

The scandal has brought out the worst in both clergy and laity. Some laity fabricated accusations in hopes of monetary gain. Some priests have arrogantly dismissed charges against them, expecting that they would be believed simply because they are priests. The laity have grown suspicious. The clergy have grown more aloof. Dioceses have found themselves trying to find a balance between pastoral response and protecting their assets. And it appears that attorneys are becoming more and more powerful in the operations of the church.

My diocese's response has reflected both sides of the crisis. Some priests have responded with great compassion and concern for victims. One woman was sharing with two priests her tale of childhood sexual abuse by a priest both of these men knew. Rather than becoming defensive, they both were deeply compassionate. One of the priests, with tears in his eyes, issued a heartfelt apology to the woman on behalf of the church he'd served faithfully.

At the same time, our parishes are now corporations. The priest is chairman of the board of directors. The motivation for such a direction is clearly to have more protection of assets in the face of lawsuits. Accused priests have become increasingly likely to hire an attorney and to attack alleged victims as mentally ill.

The idea grew in me that perhaps the time had come for me to step away from the Catholic Church for a while to get some perspective and to clear out once and for all what parts of my participation in Catholicism were motivated by fear and guilt. And so in the fall of 1999, I no longer attended Sunday Mass. I took a sabbatical from my Catholicism.

Reflection: If you are still involved with the religion of your youth, have you ever stood back from it? If you have parted company with the religion of your youth, how did this come about?

Richard Rohr observed: "The best Catholics I know usually left the Church for a while" (*Quest for the Grail.* Crossroad: New York, 1997, p. 48). My sabbatical gave me some insight into this thought. My Catholic practice had become so automatic and muddied. I now had the opportunity to observe what, if anything, I actually missed. As time passed, I realized that my problem was not with God or Jesus but with the church.

It is ironic that one of the signposts back to Mass came from an unlikely source. During my sabbatical, I constantly read, searching, I suppose, for a sign. I looked at C. S. Lewis's *Mere Christianity* (Macmillan: New York, 1943). I read Teilhard. I read Annie Dillard. No magic answers anywhere. I did find comfort in Anne Lamott's *Traveling Mercies,* her own spiritual autobiography in which she pieced together what she believes and found those realizations taking her in surprising directions as far as church was concerned. Two thoughts of Thich Nhat Hanh also took root. I have quoted them earlier but they merit repeating. In his great work *Living Buddha, Living Christ* (Riverhead Books, 1997), Hahn observed: "I do not see any reason to spend one's whole life tasting just one kind of fruit. We human beings can be nourished by the best values of many traditions" (*Living Buddha, Living Christ.* Riverhead: New York, 1995, p. 2). Right on, I thought. But then later he writes: "Learning to touch deeply the jewels of our own tradition will allow us to understand and appreciate the values of other traditions and this will benefit everyone" (*Ibid.,* p. 90). Had I really "touched deeply" the jewels of my tradition? I thought not. I began to see that there was much about my Catholicism that I did indeed treasure—some rituals, the appreciation of the mystic domain, various saints and persons of the church whom I deeply admired, a powerful tradition of service. These were some of the jewels, and I began to see that I was unwilling to cut myself off from them.

Reflection: Can you identify any jewels in the religious tradition with which you have been raised?

The final influence that pointed me back toward the church came from a surprising and unlikely source. I read a powerful and immensely disturbing book titled *Hitler's Pope* (Penguin USA, 2000). This book focused on the papacy of Pius XII and explored the manner in which the pope had failed to deal with the horror of the Nazi Holocaust. It portrayed the church as very flawed and pointed time and again to the dynamics of power and its impact on several papacies. I have to admit that my predominant thought was, "If Catholicism truly is the "One True Faith," then we are in one helluva lot of trouble!" I recalled Huston Smith's observation that the main problem with religion was people. I saw finally and clearly that Catholicism is merely one very flawed path but one that I cherish in many ways in spite of and perhaps because of its very human side.

Reflection: In what ways have you been touched, for good or for bad, by the human side of a religious tradition?

I returned to Mass after six months, taking the guidance of Robert Kennedy and viewing it from the perspective of the Japanese Tea Ceremony (*Zen Spirit, Christian Spirit: The Place of Zen in Christian Life.* Continuum: New York, 1995).

Three other significant events have occurred of late. One occurred a year ago. I had visited with a friend who works as a Franciscan missionary, and he had shared experiences on a retreat he'd made. He would go for walks in the desert and would encounter objects which bore significance to him. He'd focus his meditations for the day on that object. One day, he'd actually come upon a crucifix in the desert! I was most impressed. For some years I'd walked home from my office on Good Friday. Sort of a pilgrimage. In any case, on this particular Good Friday, I took inspiration from my friend's experience. I was sure I'd encounter some object of great significance (thereby forgetting what I'd learned about the spontaneous nature of mystical experiences!) I began to drive myself crazy. Was it that telephone pole I was supposed to notice? This piece of trash? Good grief! Maybe I'll miss it completely!

After about ninety minutes of this, I gave up. No sign would come my way. At that very instant, I was passing by an apartment complex. Walking into the complex was my friend Delia Gomez, a woman whom I greatly admire for her efforts on the border helping immigrants and the poor. I stopped to exchange pleasantries with her. After I continued on my way,

I realized, Delia was the sign! My spirituality tends to become too introverted, and God is reminding me to make room for people on my spiritual journey. So, once again, I received what I sought, but only after letting go.

A second powerful spiritual experience occurred when my wife and I traveled to Ireland, the land of my ancestors. Years ago, my brother and I had encouraged my parents to take a trip to Ireland, something my mother in particular really wanted to do. But it never happened. There were relatives to be cared for. Then my dad had his strokes. Then my mom died. The trip never happened. So I felt her presence on this trip.

I'd decided that I wanted to visited some churches in Ireland on my mother's behalf and that I would light some candles for her and a few other loved ones. These church visits had impact beyond what I'd imagined. I felt something very deep stirring in me in response to what I witnessed. I even managed to attend one Mass in Killkenny, where I swear the priest celebrating the Mass was a reincarnation of Barry Fitzgerald, the wonderful Irish priest in the film *Going My Way.*

During this time, Ireland was facing the threat of foot and mouth disease, an illness that hits animals and greatly threatened Ireland's two biggest industries—agriculture and tourism. We became aware of just how much the Irish dealt with hardship by accepting it as "God's will." As I heard more about Irish Catholic faith, I was put back in touch with my mother's faith. I was moved by the quiet, almost stoic faith which Irish people rarely talk about openly. Sounded just like my mother. These experiences made me appreciate at still deeper levels an approach to the spiritual journey that in earlier times I'd rejected.

Finally, and most recently, I have been impacted spiritually by the events of September 11, 2001. I find myself struggling with the question of where God was in the ashes of the World Trade Center, the devastation of the Pentagon, the charred field of Pennsylvania. I have heard many stories, some from friends, of events that took them away from those buildings on that morning. I am also reminded of the story of a priest, Father Mychal Judge, bending to administer last rites, only to die as the building collapsed on him. My journey of anger and confusion with God also continues.

Reflection: What spiritual impact have the events of September 11, 2001, had on you?

CHAPTER 21

The Sandwich Generation

You may notice that spiritual themes overlap many of our developmental challenges—raising children, letting them go, facing midlife. There is also a spiritual theme overlapping issue faced by what has become known as the sandwich generation.

This is the generation roughly within my own age group—the generation also known as the baby boomers. This generation is now caught between two other generations—our children and our parents. The job of raising our children overlaps or, in many cases, winds down as we take up the task of caring for our aging parents. This job in turn culminates in the pain-filled task of letting our parents go.

Reflection: Are you coping with or have you coped with aging parents?

As our parents age, roles can get reversed. Old childhood wounds can resurface. We may lose the mind and spirit of a parent while the body lingers, sometimes for years.

We all want our parents to age gracefully, keep all their mental faculties intact, then die with as little pain as possible. As with so much else in life, we have no control over these outcomes.

My mother knew suffering well. In the face of tragedy, however, she maintained a steadfast faith, attending Mass for years on a daily basis and in her own quiet way conveying a deep, abiding belief in the power of prayer. Unlike me, she never questioned and never argued with her Lord, accepting what was handed to her. And so it was on the day she learned she had stomach cancer.

My dad had a stroke in May of 1994 and became a handful. When Mom started to complain of stomach pains that fall, I was certain that Dad had given her an ulcer. So when she called me from the hospital that December 7, I asked if she indeed had an ulcer. She responded very directly: "Yes. And a tumor."

Mom was eighty-one at the time, and aging gracefully. She remained an avid reader with a steel-tight memory. I hoped that this final journey would take none of that away from her. The cancer had spread within her and she decided she did not want to endure chemotherapy. I was planning a visit after the New Year, but a good friend who'd lost a daughter to cancer counseled, "Don't wait too long." So I headed back to Pennsylvania the week before Christmas. I was on my way to help Mom face her death.

On the plane back East, I prayed, asking God to not allow Mom to suffer needlessly. I knew how cancer could drag on for years and did not want Mom to face such hardship. I knew this cancer was terminal and beseeched God to not drag it out.

When I arrived at Mom's hospital room, we got to the point quickly. "I'm here to look after Dad," I said, "and to let you know, Mom, it's OK for you to go." "Well, my bags are packed," was her reply. We talked a great deal. And I waited. With each day of pain and morphine, I became angrier. "What's going on, Lord? She's such a fine person. Let her go home! Stop this pain!"

Two days before I was to head back to El Paso, Mom called early in the morning to state that she was going to beat the cancer. Later, when I got to the hospital, she'd lost some of her fight. When I asked her if she was fighting for the sake of my dad, my brother, and me, she said, "Well, of course!" at which point I said, "Mom, you've lived your whole life for other people. For once, I want you to make a decision for yourself." She paused, then said quietly, "Well, if it's for me, then I'm ready to go." But still the Lord didn't take her. And I got angrier.

The day before I left, I walked into Mom's room. She looked at me with an odd expression. "What are you still doing here?" she said. I pointed out to her that I wasn't due to leave till the following day. "Wasn't yesterday Christmas?" There was the first clue. "Mom, are you trying to stay alive through Christmas?" "Well, of course. I don't want to spoil everyone's Christmas." So there it was. Mom was in dialogue with her Lord, asking to be allowed to live through Christmas so that her beloved children and grandchildren could celebrate. What I realized in that moment was that God was indeed honoring her years of faith by granting her some choice in the hour of her departure. It was her final and perhaps best lesson on faith. And so on December 28, about fifteen minutes after one last visit with my dad, my mom went home, as she said, "to see my girls."

On the night of Mom's death, I went into the backyard and looked up to the sky, looking for her star, just as I had found John's star on my morning run at Camp Courageous. Astronomers call it Orion's Belt, but for me, there it was, Mom's star burning strong, with two smaller stars to each side. I knew she was with my sisters and that she was smiling.

Just as my parents were total opposites in personality, so their leave-taking stands in sharp contrast. As I said, my father suffered a stroke in 1994. Then another one in 1998. And another in 2000. With each stroke, he lost considerable ground and began to display more severe degrees of dementia.

In 1997, he moved to El Paso to an assisted living facility nearby. Things went reasonably well for the first year. But as dementia set in, he became argumentative and volatile. Instead of tending to personal grooming in his usually impeccable manner, he began to be unkempt. And he began to lose his past.

His dementia became more severe to the point that he was kicked out of the assisted living facility and moved to another. The topic of nursing homes was being brought up to me.

Through all this, I would pray, feeling guilty at times that I wanted relief for myself at the expense of whatever was best for my father. Yet his life had become quite empty and I wondered if he wouldn't be better off if the Lord took him. Needless to say, as he lingered in a psychological and spiritual twilight zone for the better part of two years, I was angry.

Finally, my father fell. Ironic, since that had been his greatest fear. He suffered a subdural hematoma that, the neurosurgeon told me, would be fatal unless a fairly intrusive medical procedure was undertaken. Or we could let him go. So, because my father had entrusted me with his fate when he established a living will, it was up to me.

I wish for no one else to be placed in such a position, yet I am honored and humbled that my father trusted me. He'd asked me long before his strokes not to let him linger. And so I elected to let him go. He lasted a week. I am thankful that, to the end, my father knew who I was. I expressed this last journey with him in a poem:

The Sandwich Generation

The man whom I called Dad
Was replaced some years ago
By you, Old Man.

Bit by bit
A piece at a time
You took him away
Until little of his soul was left.

Soiled.
Demented.
Putting mouthwash in his hair.
Throwing food,
Pounding tables.
Cursing.

"Who's the guy in that picture?"
"It's you, Dad."
"It is?"
"Yes. Before you and Mom were married."
"Is she gone?"
"Yes, Dad. Six years ago."

You took his body, Old Man,
Then his mind
Until all that was left
Was a child
Afraid I'd turn my back on him.

"Your birthday's next week."
"How old will I be?"
"Eighty-six, Dad."
"Eighty-six? Oh that's too long."

And so it was.
And then he fell.
The doctors wanted to drill a hole
To relieve the pressure in his head.

Let him go!
Let him go!
Doctor, do nothing!
Old Man, let him go!

"And when the time comes, Dad,
I'll take you back East
To be next to Mom."
"You will?"
"Yes, Dad. I promised you I would."
"That's good."

So there he is. Miles away.
Freed from the Old Man's grip.
Home.

And I?
I must try
To see past the feces on the floor
Past the smell of sweat and urine
Past the tears and tantrums
Past the Old Man

And remember instead
A game of catch
In a backyard
So many years ago.

Why did my father go in such a manner? I don't know. If God's will was somehow involved, I missed the point. Perhaps, as with other things in life, God is not really involved. Perhaps this is simply the price tag for medical advances. That some of us end up living too long.

Reflection: If you are elderly in some sense of the word, how does this affect your spiritual journey? If you are not elderly, what reflections do you have about growing old? How long would you like to live?

CHAPTER 22

Redemption

Perhaps the most powerful chapter of your spiritual biography centers around the theme of redemption. To be redeemed is to be lifted out of utter brokenness and restored to a degree of peace. It is the experience of converting something dark within us into something of great value. Jolande Jacobi writes: "In the negative and evil may be the hidden germs of transformation into the positive and good" (*The Way of Individuation.* Meridian: New York, 1983, p. 127). To be redeemed is greatly liberating and greatly humbling in one instant.

There are variations on the theme of redemption. We can be redeemed within the context of a religion and its rituals. We can be lifted up out of brokenness. Or we can get in touch with some dark part within and transform it into light.

These three faces of redemption are not mutually exclusive. They are tied together if we use as our metaphor *The Shawshank Redemption.* In this film, a man is wrongly accused of murder and spends years in prison before managing to escape by crawling through hundreds of yards of sewage. This indeed is how redemption can feel—being released from a prison but only after crawling through miles of sewage!

The wealth of spiritual autobiographies available to us include great stories of redemption. Saint Augustine is certainly a case in point. Other stories that have moved me include those of J. K. Huysmanns, Ann Lamott, and, of course, the story of Bill W., the cofounder of AA. Various autobiographies would confirm Richard Rohr's observation on redemption: "We don't save our soul; we *discover* it" (*The Art of Loving.* Crossroad: New York, 1992, p. 92). Perhaps this is the essence of redemption. We are lifted up from where we were headed and directed toward becoming that which we are fully capable of becoming and are meant to become. Such rescue, however, seems to come only on the heels of utter brokenness, even despair. This is the event referred to in AA as "hitting bottom." It may only be at this point that we are finally able to let go and thereby make room for redemption.

From a religious perspective, this version of redemption involves being rescued from a life of sin. This is the powerful message underlying the story of the prodigal son, a story, by the way, to which many of the men and women of AA relate.

But back to Richard Rohr's notion. If I am redeemed, I discover my soul. At what point did I discover my soul? I think it was at the end of *Return of the Jedi* as I felt tears rising within me as I watched the redemption of Anakin Skywalker (aka Darth Vader).

Reflection: If you have had a redemptive experience, can you pinpoint its onset?

The experience of redemption is a fragile one. I am fully aware that I am one drink away from being cast back down into the pit. So what we receive needs to be protected and nurtured. We should never take such gifts for granted.

Reflection: If you have had a redemptive experience, how have you taken care of this gift?

Conclusion

I summarize where I am in my journey at this point with these observations:

1. I seem to be rediscovering something of value in the roots of my Catholicism.
2. I see value in simple faith and in stoic faith.
3. I continue to find great value in what I understand of Zen Buddhism. Thoughts on suffering and on attachments have been especially impactful.
4. My journey has been enriched by Jewish theologians and mystics.
5. I have major issues with the organization of the Catholic Church. While I have encountered some truly wonderful people serving the church, I find the organization to be focused heavily on power and to be sexually neurotic.
6. I continue to need to work on horizontal spirituality, i.e., spirituality that involves community and service.
7. I continue to wrestle with serious doubts about the impact of prayer and the existence and nature of an afterlife. I continue to experience powerful outcomes to my prayers yet continue, like Saint Thomas the Apostle, to look for signs.
8. I am humbled to see just how much anger and outcry has been a part of my relationship with the God of my understanding. He/She has been very patient.

Reflection: Can you summarize where you are spiritually right now?

Rabbi David Wolpe sums up well what I believe to be true at this point: "The search for faith in one's life is a battle, alternately infuriating and enchanting, wonderful and bitterly disappointing. But part of being human is asking the most important questions that confront us, asking them again and again, not letting them go until we figure out what it means to be a human being, why we were put here, whether we were put here for any reason at all" (*The Healer of Shattered Hearts: A Jewish View of God.* Penguin: New York, 1990, pp. 20–21).

I have a hunch. Is it possible, as I crash around in the bushes seeking God, that He/She is standing right nearby the entire time, waiting patiently for me? Perhaps the day will come when I finally turn around and learn once and for all what C. S. Lewis saw years ago:

> So it was you all along.
> Everyone I ever loved, it was you.
> Everyone who ever loved me, it was you.
> Everything decent or fine that ever happened to me,
> Everything that made me reach out and try to be better,
> It was you all along.

The Inspirational Writings of C. S. Lewis.
New York: Inspirational Press, by arrangement
with Harcourt Brace, 1987, p. 288

Reflection: Where would you like to be spiritually a year from now?

Annotated Bibliography

What follows are some suggestions for further reading. Included are readings on some but not all of the topics we covered.

Introduction to Spiritual Autobiographies

Amy Mandeleker and Elizabeth Powers, eds., *Pilgrim Souls: A Collection of Spiritual Autobiographies* (Touchstone: New York, 1999). This is an excellent survey of spiritual autobiographies, excerpts ranging from Socrates and King David to Flannery O'Conner and Annie Dillard. It would be hard not to find a kindred soul among the excerpts.

A Selection of Spiritual Autobiographies

Thomas Merton, *The Seven Storey Mountain* (Harvest Books: Orlando, FL, 1999). This may be the best known of spiritual autobiographies and is the story of Father Merton's journey from man of the world to Trappist Monk.

C. S. Lewis, *Mere Christianity* (HarperSanFrancisco, 2001). Lewis has certainly become one of the most popular spiritual writers. This work portrays his intellectual awakening to the tenets of Christianity.

Henri Nouwen, *Seeds of Hope: A Henri Nouwen Reader* (Doubleday: New York, 1997). Most of Father Nouwen's writings have strong autobiographical elements to them. This work provides an overview. Other works of his with strong autobiographical themes include *Road to Daybreak* and *The Inner Voice of Love* (Doubleday: New York, 1998).

Rick Bragg, *All Over but the Shoutin'* (Vintage Books: New York, 1998). This book might at first glance not seem to be the stuff of spirituality. But it includes Mr. Bragg's struggles with organized religion and most especially is a story of how his mother faced suffering with courage and dignity.

Anne Lamott, *Traveling Mercies: Some Thoughts on Faith* (Anchor Books: New York, 2000). Ms. Lamott shares her own journey in a most endearing manner. She gives hope to those of us who stumble and who have battled addiction.

Other favorite spiritual autobiographies have included Annie Dillard's *Pilgrim at Tinker Creek* (Harper Perennial: New York, 1998), Terry Tempest Williams' *Refuge* (Vintage Books: New York, 1992), Carl Jung's *Memories, Dreams, Reflections* (Vintage Books: New York, 1989), Loren Eiseley's *All the Strange Hours: The Excavation of a Life* (Bison Books: Omaha, NE, 2000), and Louise Fisher's collection of the writings of Mahatma Gandhi *The Essential Gandhi: An Anthology of His Writings on His Life, Work and Ideas* (Vintage Books: New York, 1983).

On Suffering

The suggested readings here provided no answers but point toward good questions.

Viktor Frankl, *Man's Search for Meaning* (Washington Square Press: New York, 1998). This classic work provides the essentials of Frankl's theory on meaning as well as Frankl's experiential context for this theory. A more theoretical exploration of Frankl's theory of logotherapy can be found in his *The Doctor and the Soul* (Vintage Books: New York, 1986).

Harold Kushner, *When Bad Things Happen to Good People* (Avon: New York, 1997). Another classic exploration of making sense of suffering.

William Safire, *The First Dissident: The Book of Job in Today's Politics* (Random House: New York, 1993). Job is certainly one of the most interesting and ignored figures in sacred writings. Safire's examination of his story is thought-provoking and, for those of us who struggle with spiritual anger, comforting.

Bridges from Psychology to Spirituality and Back

Morton Kelsey, *Companions on the Inner Way* (Crossroad: New York, 1979). Written as a guide for spiritual direction, this book is valuable to anyone trying to accompany persons on spiritual journeys. While written from a Christian perspective, its insights are ecumenical.

Henri Nouwen, *The Wounded Healer* (Image Books: New York, 1979). A good introduction to the archetype that is also an essential feature of the bridge.

Sheldon Kopp, *If You Meet the Buddha on the Road, Kill Him* (Bantam Books: New York, 1988). Many of Sheldon Kopp's writings are spiritual in nature with an emphasis on integrating Eastern thought into psychological practice. This book is one of his best known. Also recommended is *End to Innocence: Life without Illusions* (Bantam Books: New York, 1983).